ASTROLOGY
MINI BOOK

**Find your sign and
your true self!**

Trish MacGregor

Adams Media Corporation
Holbrook, Massachusetts

Copyright ©2000, Adams Media Corporation.

An Everything Series Book.
"Everything" is a trademark of Adams Media Corporation.

Published by Adams Media Corporation
260 Center Street, Holbrook, MA 02343
www.adamsmedia.com

ISBN: 1-58062-385-9

Printed in Canada.

J I H G F E D C B A

Library of Congress Cataloging-in-Publication Data
available from the publisher.

Cover illustrations by Barry Littmann.
Interior illustrations by Barry Littmann and Kathie Kelleher.

This book is available at quantity discounts for bulk purchases.
For information, call 1-800-872-5627.

Contents

INTRODUCTION

Astrology's Ancient Origins to Present Day

The origin of astrology is so intimately entwined with the genesis of astronomy that it's nearly impossible to separate the two. Think of them as Siamese twins born some 32,000 years before the birth of Christ, when Cro-Magnon man kept track of celestial happenings and the passage of seasons by carving notches into bones.

It's not known, of course, whether Cro-Magnon man related celestial events to his daily life. What *is* known, however, is that most scholars agree that astrology probably dates back to the Chaldeans of Mesopotamia, who lived 3000 years before Christ was born. These people built tremendous watch towers called ziggurats, from which their priests observed celestial movements. Many of the megaliths across Europe, of which Stonehenge is the best known, are also thought to have been celestial observatories.

Astrology was practiced among the ancient Egyptians, in ancient China around 2000 B.C., and in ancient Greece. From Greece, its practice traveled to Rome, where Augustus, the first emperor, became an avid believer.

Modern astrology actually began about 200 A.D. when Claudius Ptolemaeus (Ptolemy), the most important astronomer of the time, wrote his four-volume book on the subject, *Tetrabiblos*. He regarded astrology and astronomy as adjuncts to each other. Much of

astrological practice today is based on
Ptolemy's material.

During astrology's long journey from
Ptolemy to the close of the twentieth century, it
has been ridiculed by scientists and con-
demned by Christians. Saint Augustine, a fourth-
century bishop, contended that if you believed
in astrology, then you were denying the power
of God. This attitude prevailed with such force
that the practice of astrology nearly vanished
until the twelfth century, when scholars started
translating Arabic texts on the subject.

It was during this time that the Arabic
parts in astrology began to surface. These included thirty-
two points in a chart that
were believed to be significant in horoscope inter-
pretation. They ranged from

the part of fortune to the parts of life, death, sickness, and marriage.

In 1610, Galileo explained that he'd discovered new stars and four new planets, which ancient astrologers had not accounted for. The planets were later found to be four of Jupiter's moons, but the damage had been done. In 1660, Copernicus came along and said that Earth wasn't the center of the universe, that the Earth, in fact, revolved around the sun. With each successive scientific pronouncement—Newton, Darwin, Gregor Mendel—astrology was

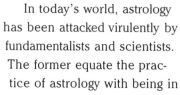

driven farther underground and into greater disrepute.

In today's world, astrology has been attacked virulently by fundamentalists and scientists. The former equate the practice of astrology with being in league with Satan. The latter consider astrology to be irrelevant.

One organization in particular, CSICOPS (Committee for the Scientific Investigation of Claims of the Paranormal) was formed specifically to disprove astrology. The article that set the stage for CSICOPS was called "Objections to Astrology" and was published in the organization's magazine *The Humanist*. It was signed by 186 scientists that included eighteen Nobel prize winners, all of them disturbed by the exploitation of a public that believed astrology and astronomy were synonymous.

CHAPTER 1

Sun Signs

An Overview

The Sun symbolizes the ego and how it expresses itself. The sign in which your sun falls influences the goals you choose and how you accomplish those goals.

I have included general comments on health issues that might concern each sun sign and a physical description. An individual's physical appearance, however, is usually influenced more strongly by the ascendant or rising sign, which rules the first house of self.

The twelve sun signs are divided roughly by months, but because those divisions don't follow the months exactly, you may have been born on the cusp between two signs. If you were, then read the interpretations for both signs. If, for instance, you were born on April 19, the cutoff date for Aries, also read the interpretation for Taurus, because some of those attributes probably apply to you.

The signs are grouped according to triplicities (the elements) and quadruplicities (types of activity and adaptability to circumstances). The elements are earth, air, fire, and water; the quadruplicities are cardinal, fixed, and mutable. Planets are also grouped according to gender.

The descriptions of sun signs are broken down into several categories: overview of the sign, women, men, kids, compatibility, romance, work, finances, physical, and spirituality. Under compatibility, a safe rule of thumb is that a given sun sign usually gets along with signs that are sextile—sixty degrees away or one sign removed on either side.

Table 1: Triplicities

Air Signs (masculine): Gemini, Libra, Aquarius

Air signs deal with mental abilities and intellectual attributes. Geminis generally have an ease for acquiring, using, and communicating information. Libras weigh, balance, and compare information. Aquarians apply what they know to universal principles.

Earth Signs (feminine): Taurus, Virgo, Capricorn

Practicality is the hallmark of earth signs. The pragmatism manifests in the houses where earth planets are found. In Taurus, the practicality may show up as an ability to accumulate and manage material resources. In Virgo, this talent is evident in intellectual matters, in a practical application and use of material resources. Capricorns are terrific organizers and managers of financial and material resources.

Table 1: Triplicities (continued)

Fire Signs (masculine): Aries, Leo, Sagittarius

The fire triplicity is characterized by aggression and some kind of leadership. Aries people are good at launching new projects and ideas. Leos excel as managers, CEOs, and the central figure around whom other people gather. Sagittarians are often spiritual and philosophical leaders.

Water Signs (feminine): Cancer, Scorpio, Pisces

The focus of the water triplicity is on emotion and feeling, intuition, and deeper psychic levels of life. In Cancers, this quality usually manifests around home and family. In Scorpio, it centers around issues that involve death, joint resources, sexuality, and metaphysics. In Pisces people, this quality is most evident in a deep connection to the unconscious. The water signs are also "fruitful," because they are related to fertility.

Table 2: Quadruplicities

The qualities below apply only in a general sense and should be considered in light of the rest of the chart.

Cardinal Signs: Aries, Cancer, Libra, Capricorn

These people tend to be outgoing and social and initiate new ideas and projects. Their challenge is that they often lack endurance to see new projects to the end.

Mutable Signs: Gemini, Virgo, Sagittarius, Pisces

The hallmark here is adaptability. Mutable signs react to new situations by adapting to them. Their challenge is that they can be too changeable or malleable.

Fixed Signs: Taurus, Leo, Scorpio, Aquarius

These people resist change and continue to act and react according to fixed patterns. They have persistence, but their challenge is inflexibility and stubbornness.

Aries ♈

THE RAM (MARCH 21–APRIL 19)

Element: Fire

Quality: Cardinal

Keyword: Leadership, the pioneer spirit

Planetary Ruler: Mars

Rules: Head and face; natural ruler of first house

The pioneering spirit of the typical Aries is the same spirit that settled the United States. These are the people who set out in wagon trains across a vast wilderness more than two centuries ago because they wanted to know what was there. These are the type of people who conceived the NASA space program, who will eventually colonize other planets.

They are bold, courageous, resourceful. They always seem to know what they believe, what they want from life, and where they're going. Aries people are dynamic and aggressive in pursuing their goals, whatever they might be. They're survivors.

The challenge with this sign is persistence. Aries people sometimes lose interest if they don't see rapid results. But this tendency is compensated for by their ambition and drive to succeed. They can be argumentative, lack tact, and have bad tempers. On the other hand, their anger rarely lasts long.

Aries Woman

The bottom line with an Aries woman is don't offend or anger her. If you do, she'll never forget it and you won't see much of her after that. She'll turn her energy to someone or something else.

If you're involved with an Aries woman, the relationship had better be one of equality or she won't stick around. This isn't a woman who tolerates chauvinism.

Professionally, she's driven. She sets goals and pursues them with all the relentless energy she possesses. She's great at initi- 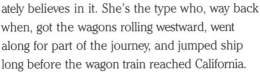 ating projects, at launching ideas, and putting things into action. But she isn't particularly good at seeing a project or idea through to its completion, unless she passion- ately believes in it. She's the type who, way back when, got the wagons rolling westward, went along for part of the journey, and jumped ship long before the wagon train reached California.

She can hold her own in most situations and certainly can compete with any man on the professional front. She exudes an aura of success and dresses to enhance that aura. In

romance, her passions are fervent and sometimes all consuming.

Aries Man

He's as bold and brash as
his female counterpart and just
as impatient and driven. Thanks
to his innate courage, he may take
up daredevil sports, but with a certain reckless-
ness. He wants to prove himself and takes
unnecessary chances and risks.

He's an excellent executive, the kind of
man who relies on his own judgment and intuition to make decisions. Like the female Aries,
he projects a successful image even if he has
failed at endeavors in the past. Some women
may find the Aries man too audacious for her
tastes, but life with him is never boring. This is
the guy who, on a whim, flies to the Caribbean
for a long weekend simply to see what's there.

Once an Aries man is smitten, watch out.
He brings his considerable energy and drive to
the relationship and pursues the woman in a
whirlwind of romance. But if the emotion isn't
reciprocated quickly, he'll be gone in a flash.

Aries Kids

On a playground filled with children, an
Aries child is easy to pick out. He's organizing
the others and directing the action. Or he and
several of his cronies are out exploring,
turning over rocks in a search of interesting bugs.

An Aries child, just like the adult
Aries, fears nothing, which is sure to
send an over-protective parent into
occasional fits. When he doesn't get
his own way, watch out for an explosion of
temper. But when he's feeling good, he's fun,
loving, and tender.

Compatibility

Aries, because it's a fire
sign, is often attracted to other
fire signs—Sagittarius or Leo.

But generally, unless aspects in the chart indicate otherwise, romance with another fire
sign can be explosive. Aries gets along well
with air signs—Gemini, Libra, Aquarius—or a
sign that's sextile (60 degrees) or trine (120
degrees) from Aries. Sometimes, an earth
sign helps ground all that Aries energy. In
chart comparisons, a Venus or moon in Aries
in the other person's chart would indicate
compatibility.

Romance

Watch out! Romance with an
Aries is an experience you don't
quickly forget. Man or woman,
these people are all passion and fire.

They often form impulsive, rash attachments, but they don't hold back emotionally. They need to know, however, that they're appreciated and loved in return.

Romance with an Aries means movement, activity, and being on the go to museums, movies, midnight walks by the ocean, good food in good restaurants, and more exotic things like hang gliding, parachuting, or rock climbing. Remember that these people are fearless and they bring that courage to their relationships.

Work

An Aries excels at anything in which leadership ability is paramount. They like giving orders and they're terrific at delegating responsibilities. They have numerous ideas and want to put them all into effect yesterday. As a fire sign, they pour energy into whatever they do. They aren't particularly interested in having power over others. They simply want the power to do what they want without restriction.

Finances

No two ways about it: Aries people spend money as fast as it comes in. An Aries knows something should be tucked away, but retirement seems such a long ways off and besides, money always comes in when needed! The challenge for an Aries is to develop the habit of saving.

Physical Aries

These people often have ruddy complexions, arched brows, narrow chins, and in men, profuse body hair. An Aries requires adequate rest and good nutrition to replenish all the energy he burns. They shouldn't eat much red meat and will benefit from herbs that belong to this particular sign: mustard, eyebright, and bay.

Since Aries rules the head and face, these areas are considered to be the weakest parts of the body. Common ailments are tension headaches, dizziness, and skin eruptions.

Spirituality

Aries is likely to sample a little of everything before deciding on which spiritual belief fits best. He might live in an ashram, delve into paganism, or even try out a more conventional religion. While involved with a particular spiritual path, he will be passionate about it. But unless his passion is sustained, an Aries will eventually get bored and move on to something new.

Notable Aries People

Marlon Brando
Richard Chamberlain
Howard Cosell
Betty Ford
Aretha Franklin
Erica Jong
Henry Mancini
Steve McQueen
Eddie Murphy

Leonard Nimoy
Laurence Olivier
Debbie Reynolds
Diana Ross
Rod Steiger
Gloria Steinem
Spencer Tracy
Vincent Van Gogh

Taurus ♉

THE BULL (APRIL 20–MAY 20)

Element: Earth

Quality: Fixed

Keywords: Endurance, perseverance, stubbornness

Planetary Ruler: Venus

Rules: Neck, throat, cervical vertebrae; natural ruler of second house

While Aries is out pioneering and discovering new lands, Taurus is settling it, cultivating the land, and using his resources for practical purposes. His stubbornness and determination keep him around for the long haul on any project or endeavor.

These individuals are the most stubborn in the zodiac. They are also incredibly patient, singular in their pursuit of goals, and determined to attain what they want. Although they lack versatility because of the fixed nature of the sign, they compensate for it by enduring whatever they have to in order to get what they want. Long after other contestants have fallen out of the race Taurus individuals are still in the running. As a result, they often win when others fail.

Most Taureans enjoy being surrounded by nice things. They like good art, good music, and many have considerable musical ability. They also have a talent for working with their hands—gardening, woodworking, and sculpting.

It takes a lot to anger a Taurus person, but once you do, clear out. The "bull's rush" can be fierce. But thanks to Venus ruling this sign, Taurus people are usually sensual and romantic. They are also physically oriented individuals who take pride in their bodies.

Taurus Woman

She's loyal and dedicated to whatever she loves most. The place around which her life is centered reflects her particular tastes in art, color, and decor. She enjoys beauty, whatever its guise. If she's into clothing, then she dresses well and tastefully. If sports and physical activity are her passion, she pursues them diligently and with tremendous patience.

Since the Taurus woman is Venus-ruled, she's a romantic. Court her with flowers, moonlit walks on a beach, poetry. She's a generous, ardent lover who probably has a love of music. She may even play an instrument or sing. If you want to change her opinion on something, go about it in a gentle way. Don't ever back her into a corner. She'll dig in her heels and refuse to budge.

As an earth sign, she likes to putter in the garden and perhaps grows and cultivates herbs.

She benefits from any time spent outdoors doing something she finds pleasurable. Animals are important to her and if she has pets, they reflect her own tastes in beauty.

Taurus Man

Like his female counterpart, he works hard and patiently at what he loves. His patience and perseverance make him good at finishing what other people have started. This guy isn't impetuous. Considerable thought goes into most things that he does. It's not that he's cautious; he's merely purposeful. If he doesn't understand the reason for doing something, he won't do it and nothing you can say will change his mind.

Both men and women in this sign can be jealous and possessive. But this tendency is mitigated considerably if the Taurus man knows you're as sincere as he is. He may

have a deep connection with nature and the
natural world that manifests in camping and
solo sports. If he works out in a gym, he
probably does it alone without a trainer. He
may be into yoga, alternative medicine, and
health foods.

His romantic nature may not always show
up in flowers and gifts, but he does others
things that tell you he cares. In return, he
enjoys a good massage, likes having his neck
rubbed, and melts in front of a fireplace.

Taurus Kids

This kid may be a loner or prefers one or
two friends to a group of buddies. When she
plays, she has fixed ideas about how the play
should proceed. She has her own
script and won't be persuaded to
change it unless she understands
the reason why and agrees it's the
best way to play the game. When she

gets tense, it shows up in the neck area. She benefits from massage and physical exercise.

Encourage Taurus kids to explore their own creativity, whether it's art, music, drama, or simply an appreciation of these things. They benefit from the rhythms of nature, from being outside and engaged in physical activity.

Forget time out for a Taurus child; he or she will simply outwait you. Better to explain what you object to and why, then ask for a promise not to repeat the act again.

Compatibility

Conventional wisdom says that we're better off with people who share the same element we do or with people who feed our element (earth with water, for instance). This makes Taurus compatible with other earth signs (Virgo and Capricorn) and with the water signs.

Quite often, Taureans are fatally attracted to Scorpios, their polar opposites. Although their elements, earth and water, should make them compatible, it tends to be superficial. Beneath the surface, they are probably at war with each other.

Romance

In romance with a Taurus, a lot goes on under the surface, out of sight. They're subtle and quiet about what they feel. Once they fall, they fall hard and their fixed natures simply won't allow them to give up. As a Venus-ruled sign, Taureans are true sensualists and romantic lovers. Their romantic attachments ground and stabilize them.

Work

They excel at work that requires persistence, stability, and relentless drive. They're able to take abstract ideas and make them concrete and practical. This means they're good at behind-the-scenes work, especially if the work is artistically creative—writing, costume design, gourmet cooking, musical composition, or anything to do with nature. You won't find a more tireless worker in the zodiac.

Finances

Despite the Taurean need for material security, they enjoy spending money. But the spending is rarely frivolous because Taurean tastes are quite specific and usually refined. Books, art, travel, and shamanic workshops may offer security for the Taurus.

Physical Taurus

They are recognizable by their necks, which are often thick and sturdy. They tend to be attractive people with broad foreheads and many retain their youthful appearances long after the rest of us begin to show our age. They benefit from a daily regimen of physical exercise and should be moderate in their consumption of fattening foods. This, of course, is undoubtedly true for all signs, but particularly true for the slower metabolism of the bull.

Spirituality

Taurus, due to the fixed, earth temperament of the sign, often seeks spiritual answers in nature. While camping, hiking, or engaged in some sort of physical activity outside, he or she connects with the deeper levels of self. Music and the arts can have the same effect on a Taurus.

Notable Taurus People

Candice Bergen

Frank Capra

Cher

Ulysses S. Grant

Joseph Heller

Audrey Hepburn

Dennis Hopper

Reggie Jackson

Soren Kierkegaard

Shirley MacLaine

Ann-Margaret

Rod McKuen

Maureen O'Sullivan

Michelle Pfeiffer

Katherine Anne Porter

Barbra Streisand

Gemini ♊

THE TWINS (MAY 21–JUNE 21)

Element: Air

Quality: Mutable

Keyword: Versatility

Planetary Ruler: Mercury

Rules: Hands, arms, lungs, nervous system; natural ruler of the third house

After Aries and Taurus have discovered and cultivated the new land, Gemini ventures out to see what else is there and seizes upon new ideas that will help their communities expand. The innate curiosity of this sign keeps these people on the move.

Geminis, because they're ruled by Mercury, tend to use the rational, intellectual mind to explore and understand their personal worlds. They need to answer the single burning question in their minds: Why? This applies to most facets of their lives, from the personal to the impersonal. This need to know may send them off to foreign countries, particularly if the sun is in the ninth house, where they can explore other cultures and traditions.

These individuals are fascinated by relationships and the connections among people, places, and objects. Their rational analysis of everything, from ideas to relationships, drives them as nuts as it drives everyone else around them. When this quality leads them into an exploration of psychic and spiritual realms, it grounds them.

Geminis are changeable and often moody. Their symbol, the twins, means they are often at odds with themselves, the mind demanding one thing, the heart demanding the opposite. To someone else, this internal conflict often manifests as two very different people; as a significant other, you may reach a point where you wonder which twin you're living with.

In romance, the heart of a Gemini is won by a seduction of the mind.

Gemini Woman

At first glance, she seems to be all over the place. She can talk on any number of topics and sounds like she knows what she's talking about, until you discover that her knowledge on most things is superficial. But if you hit one of her passions, her knowledge is deep and thorough. She excels at communication; the form this talent takes depends on other aspects in her chart.

In her twenties, she tends to be flirtatious and flighty, unable or unwilling to commit to a relationship. On the one hand, this girl loves her freedom; on the other, relationships are important to her. If she marries young, she may marry at least twice. In her thirties and forties, she begins to settle in. By this time she has made a kind of peace with herself. She has a better understanding of her moods, needs, and emotions. By fifty, the Gemini woman knows who she is; now she must begin living that truth.

If you want to change this woman's attitude or opinion, you have to prove that your attitude or opinion is more logical. Remember that her concept of logic may differ from yours.

Gemini Man

He's quick, witty, enigmatic. Just when you think you've got him figured out, he says or does something that blows your concept of who he is. Don't expect a courtship from this guy; he doesn't possess the sensual appreciation of beauty that a Taurus man has. But if you appeal to his intellect, if you court him mentally, he might dedicate his next book to you.

Like his female counterpart, the Gemini man often seems to be two people inhabiting one body. One twin is attentive to your every need and whim; he's solicitous. But the other twin could care less. You won't change this particular quality, you simply have to learn to live with it.

The Gemini man makes a good editor, writer, or orator. He may hold down two jobs and is certainly capable of working on more than one project at a time. Once he commits to something, whether it's a profession or a relationship, he needs to know that he is appreciated.

Gemini Kids

As toddlers, their personalities are marked by impatience. They don't bother learning to crawl; they're trying to walk as soon as their legs are strong enough to support them. Once they learn to communicate, watch out. They challenge you at every step with questions. Why this, why that, why why why.

These kids are as precocious as Aries children, but inconsistent in the way they express it. Some days a Gemini leads the neighborhood kids into anarchy; the next day he or she might keep company with a book, a microscope, or a pet. They like the furry warmth and security of a pet and enjoy observing how animals live on a daily basis.

As a parent, you can forget trying to pigeon-hole your Gemini child. It just isn't going to happen. So accept the fact, provide a learning environment in which your Gemini can explore who and what he or she is, and be prepared for a wild ride.

Compatibility

Geminis are social enough to get along with just about anyone on a superficial basis. They feel most at home with other air signs, particularly Aquarians, whose minds are as quick. They also get along with Sagittarius, their polar opposites in the zodiac, who share some of the same attributes. Again, though, these are broad generalizations. For compatibility purposes, compare the individual charts.

Romance

Geminis love first with their minds. Even a relationship that begins primarily because of a sexual attraction won't last if there's no mental camaraderie. Quite often, Geminis seek friendship first with the opposite sex and once a mental rapport is established, the friendship deepens to love. They can be quite fickle in their affections, sometimes carrying on simultaneous relationships. But once their hearts are won, they love deeply.

Work

Geminis excel in any line of work that provides diversity. It doesn't matter if it's with the public or behind the scenes, as long as it isn't routine. They make good counselors because one of the twins is always willing to listen. Their love of language gives them a talent for the written word. Acting, politics, libraries, research: all of these fields fit Gemini. The bottom line is simple: Boredom to a Gemini is like death.

Finances

How a Gemini handles money depends on which twin holds the purse strings—the spend-thrift or the tightwad. Either way, Geminis enjoy spending money on the things they love, such as books, movies, theater, and travel. To paraphrase the old Jefferson Airplane song, these things feed their heads.

Physical Gemini

They generally are slender and wiry people, filled with nervous energy. All this energy can be difficult to rein in sometimes, particularly on nights when they work late and their heads race with ideas. Geminis benefit from breaks in their established routines and need physical exercise to ground their thoughts. They are prone to respiratory and nervous ailments.

Spirituality

Geminis are so restless mentally that they generally don't do well within organized religions, unless they've chosen that path for themselves. They sample spiritual belief systems the way other people sample new foods. Once they find a spiritual path that makes sense to them, they generally stick with it.

Notable Gemini People

Joan Collins

Jacques Cousteau

Clint Eastwood

Sigmund Freud

Dashiell Hammett

Susan Hayward

Lillian Hellman

Bob Hope

Hubert Humphrey

John F. Kennedy

Stan Laurel

Paul McCartney

Marilyn Monroe

Joe Namath

Whitley Streiber

Orson Welles

Cancer ♋

THE CRAB (JUNE 22–JULY 22)

Element: Water

Quality: Cardinal

Keyword: Nurturing, emotional drive

Planetary Ruler: Moon

Rules: Breasts, stomach, digestive system; natural ruler of the fourth house

Now that the first three signs have discovered, settled, and expanded their new land, the Cancer comes along and tames it. Civilizes it. These people need roots, a place or even a state of mind, that they can call their own. They need a safe harbor, a refuge, to retreat for solitude.

Imagination, sensitivity, and the nurturing instinct characterize this sign. Cancerians are generally gentle and kind people, unless they're hurt.

Then they become vindictive and sharp-spoken. They forgive easily, but rarely forget.

Cancerians tend to be affectionate, passionate, and even possessive at times. As parents, they might be over-protective. As spouses or significant others, they may smother their mates with love and good intentions.

Emotionally, Cancers act and react in the same way the crab moves—sideways. They avoid confrontations and usually aren't comfortable in discussing what they feel. They're reluctant to reveal who they are and sometimes hide behind their protective urges, preferring to tend to the needs of others rather than to their own needs. They're intuitive and sometimes quite psychic. Experience flows through them emotionally.

Cancers are often moody and always changeable; their interests and social circles shift constantly. Once a

Cancer trusts you, however, he lets you in on his most private world.

Cancer Woman

At first she seems enigmatic, elusive. She's so changeable in her moods that you never know where you stand with her. Beneath her gentle and sympathetic nature, beneath her bravado, she's scared of being pinned down and insecure about who she is.

She needs roots—her own home, preferably near water—but she can establish a base of operation anywhere. She nurtures everything—animals, her own children, waifs and orphans of all shapes, sizes, and species. This woman is emotion distilled into its purest form. She feels first, then thinks. Sometimes she's a psychic sponge who absorbs every emotion around her.

If she doesn't have children of her own, she probably has some sort of connection with children. Or her animals or people in need are her children. Somehow, her nurturing instinct finds expression.

Cancer Man

Like the female Cancer, the male has liquid eyes that communicate a kind of forlorn nostalgia for what has passed. He's kind, affectionate, and nurturing, but only to a point. When he feels his personal space has been infringed upon, he retreats just like the crab—rapidly to the side. Then he buries himself in sand by retreating to his special place—his own home, his RV, his tent, whatever his refuge is. Like the female Cancer, he is often nurturing and gets along well with kids.

This guy is hard to figure. Sometimes he courts you with flowers and candlelight; other times he's sacked out on the couch lost in his own gloom. Your best course of action is to let him be. Don't prod him when he's in this kind of mood. You won't get anywhere even if you do.

If he's interested in spiritual issues, chances are he's in deep. In this sign, you're likely to find psychic healers and clairvoyants, people who use their intuition in highly developed and sophisticated ways.

Cancer Kids

The Cancerian youngster definitely listens to a different drummer. Don't expect loquacious explanations about what your Cancerian is feeling. If she's in the mood she might tell you how so-and-so hurt her feelings today at school. But if she's not in the mood, nothing you can say will prod her to explain.

This kid is often dreamy. She would rather watch TV or read a book than run around outside, unless the activity or sport happens to interest her. In a group, she's likely to take the easy way out and go along with the crowd. Or remain completely passive about the situation, hiding inside of "I don't know," or, worse, "I don't care."

The Cancerian child needs to feel that he or she is an integral part of the family unit and is appreciated. As a parent, your best route to communication with a Cancer child is acceptance and gentle prodding.

Compatibility

On the surface, Scorpio and Pisces, as the other water signs, would seem to be the most compatible with a Cancer. But Scorpio's intensity might swallow up Cancer's innate gentleness, and the duality of Pisces probably would drive a Cancer person crazy. Earth signs—Taurus, Virgo, Capricorn—are particularly good for Cancers with Taurus and

Virgo as the preferred because they are both
sextile to Cancer.

Romance

Cancers can be evasive when it
comes to romance. They flirt, they're
coy, and all the while they're feeling
their way through the maze of their own
emotions. They enjoy entertaining at home
because it's where they feel most comfortable, surrounded by all that's familiar to them. Some
Cancers dislike the courtship of romance altogether
and prefer to get right down to the important questions: Are we compatible? Do we love each other?

To live with and love a Cancer, you have to
accept the intensity of their emotions and their
imaginations.

Work

Cancers may be happiest when
they work out of their own homes.

Due to the intensity of their feelings, they do well in medicine working directly with patients. For the same reason they also make good psychic healers, counselors, and psychologists. Teaching kids, running a daycare center, or even taking care of other people's homes are also good for the Cancerian personality.

Finances

Cancers aren't lavish spenders except when it comes to their homes and families. Then, nothing is too expensive. Otherwise, they tend to be big savers. As kids, they stash their allowance in cookie jars; as adults, they stick their money in long-term CDs.

Physical Cancer

This sign is more recognizable than some of the others because of the roundness of the face. The entire body, in fact, may be rounded, though not necessarily overweight. Cancerians benefit from water sports, a day at the beach, or anything having to do with water. If they have hangups about their earlier lives, particularly childhood, hypnosis might be a good way to dislodge and work through the past. It's important that a Cancer doesn't cling to past hurts and injuries, as these emotions eventually lodge in the body and create health problems.

Spirituality

Introspection is key with Cancers and it doesn't matter if it's provided in the guise of organized religion or some New Age belief system. When they feel the rightness of a particular set of beliefs, they stick with it, explore it, and draw on their innate intuition to understand it.

Notable Cancer People

Dan Aykroyd

James Brolin

Mel Brooks

Tom Cruise

Olivia de Havilland

Harrison Ford

Merv Griffin

Franz Kafka

Helen Keller

George Orwell

Jason Robards

Linda Ronstadt

Ringo Starr

Meryl Streep

Donald Sutherland

Henry David Thoreau

Leo ♌

THE LION (JULY 23–AUGUST 22)

Element: Fire

Quality: Fixed

Keyword: Action, power

Planetary Ruler: Sun

Rules: Heart, back, and spinal cord; natural ruler of the fifth house

Yes, Leos roar. They love being the center of attention and often surround themselves with admirers. To remain in the proud kingdom of a Leo, their admirers have to think like he thinks, believe what he believes, and hate and love who he hates and loves. To a Leo, this is loyalty. In return, Leo the king offers generosity, warmth, and compassion.

Leos have an innate dramatic sense and life is definitely their stage. Their flamboyance and personal magnetism extend to every facet of their lives. They seek to succeed and make an impact in every situation. It is no surprise that the theater and allied arts fall under the rulership of Leo.

Don't ever argue to change the opinions and beliefs of a Leo. As a fixed sign, they stand firm in their belief systems. They have found what works for them and don't understand why their beliefs may not work for someone else.

In general, they are optimistic, honorable, loyal, and ambitious.

Leo Woman

She's up front about what she feels and invariably is disappointed when she finds that other people may not be as forthright. You'll never have to guess where you stand with a Leo woman, unless there's something in the aspects of her chart that say otherwise. She loves flattery, romantic courtships, and is an ardent lover.

The Leo woman exudes confidence and because of it, other people place their trust in her. She needs to be at the helm in her work-place—a manager will do but a CEO would be better. She dislikes playing second fiddle on any level.

In a marriage, don't expect her to be content with staying home, unless she's running her business from there. If she's a mother, she's not just a mother. She has a career, hobbies, and passions. She may be involved somehow with children even if she doesn't have her own, because Leo rules children.

She likes nice clothes and probably dresses with flair and style in bright, bold colors. Remember, she's an actress and adept at creating certain impressions and moods through the way she looks and acts. She likes order in her world, but it has to be her order.

Leo Man

Give him center stage and he's at his best; tell him what to do and he's at his worst. Once you accept that about the Leo man, he's easy to get along with because you really want to like this guy. He's warm, outgoing, and fun. Kids love him because in many ways he's like they are, full of magic.

People are attracted to him because they sense his leadership abilities. They like his frankness, abundant energy, and ambition. If you're a Leo's significant other, get used to sharing him with his "court," whoever they might be. But rest assured that if your Leo commits to you, he means it.

Neither the male nor the female Leo do well in subservient jobs. But give them distinction and the power to command and they do it exceptionally well.

Leo Kids

As toddlers, they keep you running. Their abundant energy fuels them from sunrise to midnight, and by the time you fall into bed, you're ragged. As they mature, Leo kids are surrounded by other kids, so your house is likely to be the gathering place for your Leo's youthful tribe.

The innate generosity of this sign manifests itself early. Leo kids feel compassion toward people less fortunate than they are. They're likely to bring home strays of all shapes and sizes. They also tend to be fearless, accept every dare, and take risks that turn you gray before your time. Life with a Leo kid is never boring!

Compatibility

Another fire sign is good for a Leo simply because their energy levels are similar. Any sign that is sextile (Gemini, for instance) or trine (Aries) would be fine, too.

The polarity between Leo and Aquarius, its polar opposite sign, might elevate a Leo's consciousness to where it succeeds best: to the wider world beyond himself, the family of man.

Romance

Leos are passionate. They can also be impulsive, particularly when their egos are stroked. For the most part, Leos need to feel needed and need to know they are loved before they commit entirely. Once they're committed, everything is bigger than life and brighter than the sun. Courtship is often a series of dramatic gestures: five dozen roses that arrive at your office, an erotic call at three a.m., or a chopper ride over Manhattan.

Work

A Leo excels at work in front of the public. Actor, orator, Speaker of the House, CEO: forget the menial job for a Leo. Leos are good at teaching because the classroom becomes their stage and their students become their audience. They also tend to be good with animals and enjoy training, caring for, and loving them.

Finances

If Leo wants it, Leo buys it. If he can't afford it, he charges it. If his charge cards are maxed out, then he hocks his Rolex or his collection of baseball cards to buy it. Saving for a rainy day just isn't in the picture because for a Leo there aren't any rainy days! There are, of course, exceptions to all these generalities. A Moon in an Earth sign, combined with a Leo sun, would mitigate the flamboyance, particularly if the Moon were in Capricorn.

Physical Leo

Jacqueline Kennedy Onassis was the physical epitome of a Leo female with her compelling eyes, thick hair, and regal bearing. Leos generally benefit from low-fat diets because one of the weakest parts of their bodies is the heart. Exercise, even if on the light side, is needed to channel some of that abundant energy.

Spirituality

The Leos I've known were probably sun-worshipping pagans in past lives and now they're sampling everything else along the spectrum. Unless aspects in the chart indicate otherwise, a Leo isn't likely to stay within the confines of organized religion unless it suits him. If he does it out of obligation, then in his mind he's doing it for his kids. A Leo's greatest spiritual contributions come when he expands beyond the parameters of the self and reaches for the universal.

Notable Leo People

James Baldwin
Lucille Ball
Peter Bogdanovich
Rosalynn Carter
Geraldine Chaplin
Robert DeNiro
John Derek
Samuel Goldwyn
Dag Hammarskjold

Mata Hari
Dustin Hoffman
Mick Jagger
T.E. Lawrence
Jacqueline Kennedy
   Onassis
Ogden Nash
Roman Polanski
Arnold Schwarzenegger

Virgo ♍

THE VIRGIN (AUGUST 23–SEPTEMBER 22)

Element: Earth

Quality: Mutable

Keyword: Order, detailed, dedication

Planetary Ruler: Mercury

Rules: Intestines, abdomen, female reproductive system; natural ruler of the sixth house

The popular image of Virgos as people who are picky, critical, and compulsively tidy, is misleading. If one or all of these traits manifest obviously, the natal chart reveals other aspects that enhance this characteristic.

Virgos equal Geminis in mental quickness and agility. Due to their attention to detail, they tend to delve more deeply into subjects they study. Even though they are career-oriented people, they seem to be more interested in doing their jobs efficiently and well. They're happiest when engaged in something that bene-fits society at large. In other words, duty is important to Virgos.

They tend to be attracted to people who are intellectually stimulating or eccentric in some way. Their standards are high when it comes to romantic relationships and unless the mental con-nection exists, the relationship won't last long.

Since Virgos, like Geminis, are Mercury-ruled, they need outlets for all that nervous energy. Writing, pets, reading, and education all serve this purpose.

Virgo Woman

Physically, she's distinctive in some way—intriguing eyes, exquisite bone structure in her face, or meticulous grooming. She possesses a certain vibrancy and energy that other people sense even when she's not trying to project an image. In romance, she is attracted first when a mental spark exists. As the mental camaraderie deepens, so do her emotions.

The Virgo woman, like her male counterpart, is often insecure and tends to fret over everything. This trait usually evens out as the Virgo woman matures. It can be irritating to a significant other, particularly when her fretting turns to a constant critique of everything other people say and do.

She usually is aware of health and hygiene issues, especially when it concerns cutting-edge research. She may not always apply what she knows to her own life, but she has the knowledge.

She enjoys spending money on items like books and pieces of art that strike her fancy. She's sensitive to her surroundings, so her home is comfortable. If she's a mother, she's conscientious, tactful, and loving. She usually has a real soft spot for animals.

Virgo Man

He looks good and possesses an indisputable presence. He's mentally quick, intellectually curious, and is an excellent worker. His humor is often biting but rarely malicious.

He can be quite fussy about his personal environment. This is the kind of man who insists on having his own bathroom or, at the very least, his own side of the bathroom counter. If he cooks, then he probably is quite good at it and possessive about the kitchen while he's creating. Like the female of the sign, the Virgo man enjoys pleasant surroundings and usually owns several special items that he keeps for the sake of nostalgia.

He's prone to taking himself too seriously and benefits from any activity that forces him to lighten up. He's always hardest on himself, overly critical of what he does or doesn't do and can be quite critical of others as well. He rarely seeks praise for his efforts and in the less evolved Virgo man, won't give praise even when it's deserved.

Virgo Kids

You'd better know how to think quickly when you're around a Virgo child. They're impatient, want everything yesterday, and possess boundless energy. They love to learn and their curiosity prompts them to poke around in everything. When they feel passionate about something, they bring the full power of their being to that particular endeavor.

This child is inclined to fluctuating moods in the same way that Cancer kids are. But for a Virgo, the cause of the fluctuation originates first in the mind, rather than in the emotions. If they can't understand something, their frustration mounts until they either explode or understand the problem. Their attention span improves with age and maturity. The compassion that marks them at a young age usually deepens with time. They love animals.

As the parent of a Virgo child, provide him or her with books, learning tools, and plenty of positive feedback and praise.

Compatibility

Virgos are attracted mentally to Geminis, but sometimes find the twins a bit hard to take for the long run. The grounding present in other earth signs may seem appealing on the surface, but leave it to a Virgo to find fault with his fellow earth signs. Scorpios and Cancers may be the best bets, with the mystical Pisces a close second.

Romance

Virgos are often inscrutable in the affairs of the heart. They seem remote and quiet, then open and talkative. One moment they're glad to see you, then the next they act like they could care less. This is only the Virgo need to perfect what is. Virgos generally don't entertain romantic illusions; they see what's there in finely carved detail, like an X-ray, and then they try to improve on it. Don't take it personally. A Virgo is never harder on the people she loves than she is on herself.

Work

Virgos bring sincere striving for perfection to their work and careers. They do best when working for others—social work, in hospitals, clinics, hospice programs, with their children. The challenge in every area of a Virgo's life is to serve without self-sacrifice. Their striving for perfection compels them to evolve and change.

Finances

When Virgos are big spenders, they usually pull back at some point and question what they buy and why. What need does it fill? If they are tight with money, then something happens that impels them to loosen their hold, to spend money for enjoyment. Virgos follow an arc of evolvement toward perfection in everything they do. They analyze the patterns in their lives and seek to change those that don't work.

Physical Virgo

They usually have slender builds and are physically attractive. There may be a sharpness about their features. Since Virgos fret and worry so much, their physical ailments usually manifest first in their stomachs. Colic in infancy, stomach upsets as a youngster, ulcers as an adult. But because Virgos are generally fussy about their diet and health, they grow into their innate wisdom about their own bodies.

Spirituality

The evolved Virgo is capable of great vision and an intuition that often borders on prescience. They are likely to sample different spiritual beliefs until they find one that appeals to their eminently practical side.

Notable Virgo People

Elizabeth Ashley

Anne Bancroft

William Golding

Buddy Hackett

Michael Jackson

Elia Kazan

Ken Kesey

Jean Claude Killy

B.B. King

Stephen King

Roddy McDowall

Bill Murray

Maxwell Perkins

William Saroyan

Peter Sellers

Leo Tolstoy

Lily Tomlin

Libra ♎

THE SCALES (SEPTEMBER 23–OCTOBER 22)

Element: Air

Quality: Cardinal

Keyword: Balance

Planetary Ruler: Venus

Rules: Lower back and the diaphragm; natural ruler of the seventh house

Librans seem to come in three distinct types: those who are decisive, those who aren't, and those who seek harmony for its own sake. The typical Libra seeks to mediate and balance, to act democratically and fairly.

They love beauty in all of its guises—art, literature, classical music, opera, mathematics, and the human body. They usually are team players who enjoy debate but not argument. They're excellent strategists and masters at the power of suggestion.

Even though Librans are courteous, amiable people, never presume they're pushovers. They use diplomacy and intelligence to get what they want. They're natural romantics and flourish in enduring partnerships. They are fair-minded people, but avoid anything that is grim, crude, vulgar, and garish. Adversely afflicted, they have trouble making decisions and may lose themselves in sensual pleasures. In highly evolved Librans, the human mind is perfect in its balance and discretion.

Libra Woman

Watch out. She's a flirt who is seductive and romantic, and she bowls you over with the small luxuries she brings you. If she cooks, she probably does it well, using herbs and seasonings. She sets the mood, too, with candlelight, fresh flowers, and soft music. She's a romantic, tender lover, enjoys companionship, and flourishes in partnerships.

Her home reflects her refined tastes in art, books, and good music. She may not be extravagant and probably doesn't squander the money she has. But she derives enormous pleasure from whatever she buys. If she likes opera or the ballet, she attends regularly; these extravagances feed her soul. She may play a musical instrument and have a fondness for chess.

Libra Man

He needs companionship, just like his female counterpart, and generally works better as part of a team. But he also needs to retain his individuality in any partnership, which may be quirky at times. Once you've won his heart, he's loyal and considerate and seeks to perfect the union until it fits his idealized vision of what is possible.

He enjoys pleasant, harmonious surroundings in his work and personal environment. He often finds himself in the role of peacemaker simply because he seeks balance in all things. He shares many of the same artistic interests as his female counterpart.

A Libra man rarely expresses anger; he would rather work around whatever problems crop up. But if he lets loose, he doesn't leave anything unsaid. Every transgression and insincerity is spelled out. Although his anger passes quickly, such outbursts leave him shaken and sometimes ill because he has such an intense dislike for anything unpleasant.

Libra Kids

Chances are good that you won't find a Libra child rolling around in a sandbox or looking for bugs. Their sensibilities usually are too refined for that. The typical Libra child is more likely to be reading a book or listening to the music in the cool comfort of his or her own room.

Libra kids enjoy group activities and get along well with others kids in a group. They usually have one special friend in whom they confide. Don't be alarmed if your Libra toddler has an imaginary friend that she talks about and plays with. Many creative people had imaginary friends as youngsters. It's part of what makes their personalities different. You're better off never shouting at a Libra child. Just tell him or her what behavior you object to and extract a promise that the problem won't be repeated.

Compatibility

Librans are so sociable they can get along with just about anyone. They are most compatible with other air signs, Leo, and Sagittarius. They gravitate toward people who reflect their refined tastes and aesthetic leanings. Sometimes, an earth sign

may provide a certain grounding that a Libran
needs. Or a water sign, like Cancer, may offer a
fluidity of emotion that a Libran may lack.

Romance

Libras are drawn to beauty, whatever its form. The only thing they enjoy
as much as beauty is harmony. Even when
a relationship has gone sour, a Libra hesitates to
be the one who ends it. They can't stand
hurting anyone's feelings; emotional rawness is
one of those ugly realities that they don't like to
see. As a result, they may remain in a relationship longer than they should just because dishar-
mony is so distasteful. Libras seek harmony
because in their heart they know that enlighten-
ment lies at the calm dead center of the storm.

Work

The Libra's obvious choice for
a profession is an attorney or judge

because of Libra's finely tuned sense of fair play. But Librans excel in any profession that calls for an acutely balanced mind and sensitivities. They make good editors, musicians, accountants, artists, and parents. The work itself is less important in the long run than what it teaches Libra about making decisions, in spite of their ability to see all sides of an issue.

Finances

A sense of balance allows Libras to strike the right note between spender and miser. Libras tend to save, but enjoy spending when they can afford it. Most Libras know their limit.

Physical Libra

As a Venus-ruled sign, these people are usually physically

distinctive in some way—compassionate eyes or well-formed bodies. They tend to be slender, very attractive, and seem to know instinctively how to bring out the best in their companions. Since Libra rules the lower back and diaphragm, unvented emotions manifest first in those areas of the body. Libras benefit from physical exercise, particularly anything that strengthens the back and maintains general flexibility.

Spirituality

Evolved Libras understand instinctively that they must unite human duality with divine unity. They seek idealized balance, the perfect equilibrium. For some, this is accomplished within the parameters of organized religion. For others, spirituality is sought through community efforts or in their immediate family.

Notable Libra People

Lenny Bruce
Michael Douglas
Dwight Eisenhower
Graham Greene
Richard Harris
Helen Hayes
Rita Hayworth
Jim Henson
Charles A. Jayne

Buster Keaton
Ralph Lauren
Groucho Marx
Roger Moore
Mickey Rooney
Eleanor Roosevelt
Susan Sarandon
Wallace Stevens
Ben Vereen

Scorpio ♏

THE SCORPION (OCTOBER 23–NOVEMBER 21)

Element: Water

Quality: Fixed

Keyword: Regeneration, transformation

Planetary Ruler: Mars and Pluto

Rules: Sexual organs, rectum, and reproductive system; natural ruler of the eighth house

Note the sharp point at the tip of the glyph that represents this sign. Symbolically, it's the scorpion's stinger, which characterizes the biting sarcasm often associated with Scorpios. These people are intense, passionate, and strong-willed. They often impose their will on others. In less aware people, this can manifest as cruelty, sadism, and enmity; in the more evolved Scorpio, this characteristic transforms lives for the better.

Like Aries, they aren't afraid of anything. But they have an endurance that Aries lacks and it enables them to plow ahead and overcome whatever opposition they encounter.

Scorpios don't know the meaning of indifference. They tend to live in black and white worlds, dealing with either/or issues. They either approve or don't approve, agree or disagree. You're either a friend or an enemy; there are no shades of gray. Once you've gained their trust, you've won their loyalty forever, unless you hurt them or someone they love. Then they can become vindictive and may attempt to get even.

Scorpios possess an innate curiosity and suspicion of easy answers that compels them to probe deeply into whatever interests them. They dig out concealed facts and seek the meaning behind facades. Most Scorpios are exceptionally intuitive, even if they don't consciously acknowledge it. The more highly evolved people in this sign are often very psychic, with rich inner lives and passionate involvement in metaphysics.

Scorpios are excellent workers, industrious and relentless. They excel at anything associated with the eighth house—trusts and inheritances, mortuaries, psychological counselors, the occult.

Scorpio Woman

She smolders with sexuality. This is a woman who turns heads on the street, who walks into a room filled with strangers and instantly grabs attention through nothing more than the power of her presence. If you seek to win a Scorpio woman's heart, you'd better be up front and honest right from the beginning. If she ever catches you in a lie or if you hurt her, she'll cut you off cold.

She's a passionate lover and can be jealous and possessive. You won't ever figure out what she's thinking or feeling just by the expression on her face, unless she's angry and then watch out. Her rage takes many forms—an explosion, sarcasm that bites to the bone, or a piercing look that makes you shrivel inside.

If her intuition is developed, it borders on clairvoyance. This inner sense often shines forth in a Scorpio woman's striking eyes.

As a mother, the Scorpio woman is devoted, loving, and fiercely protective. She strives to create a comfortable and loving home for her kids that is also a refuge from the outside world.

Scorpio Man

Like the female of the sign, he's intense, passionate, and very private. There is always something compelling about a Scorpio man—his eyes, the way he dresses, or the enigma of his presence. He isn't just a flirt. He often comes on like a locomotive with sexual energy radiating so powerfully that he's difficult to ignore even if you aren't attracted to him.

The Scorpio man often has a marvelous talent of some kind that he pursues passionately, but which may not figure into his income. In others words, this talent is his avocation—music, art, writing, acting, astrology, tarot cards. Or, he may pour his considerable talent into nurturing his own children.

Many Scorpio men (and women) enjoy sports. They have a distinct preference for more violent sports like football and hunting. His choice of sports is sometimes a reflection of his personal struggle with emotional extremes.

Scorpio Kids

From infancy, these children are usually distinctive in some way. They form their opinions early, based on what they experience and observe. The intensity and depth of their emotions may result in outbursts of temper when they don't get their way or terrible bouts of crying when their feelings are hurt.

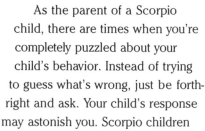

As the parent of a Scorpio child, there are times when you're completely puzzled about your child's behavior. Instead of trying to guess what's wrong, just be forthright and ask. Your child's response may astonish you. Scorpio children flourish in an environment that is rich with variety, but they definitely need their own space and sanctuary.

Compatibility

Scorpio is usually compatible with Taurus, because the signs are polar opposites and balance each other. The water of Scorpio and the earth of Taurus mix well. However, both signs are fixed, which means in a disagreement neither will give in to the other. Scorpios can be compatible with other Scorpios as long as each person understands the other's intensity and passions. Pisces and Cancer, the other two water signs, may be too weak for Scorpio's intensity, unless a comparison of natal charts indicates otherwise.

Romance

You don't know the meaning of the word intensity unless you've been involved with a Scorpio. No other sign brings such raw power to romance. The rawness probably isn't something you understand or even like very much, but there's no question that it's intricately woven through the fabric of your relationship.

The odd part is that you're never quite sure how the intensity is going to manifest: jealousy, fury, endless questions, or unbridled passion. Sometimes, the intensity doesn't have anything to do with the relationship, but with the personal dramas in the Scorpio's life. So don't try to figure it out. If you're in for the long haul, then accept your Scorpio the way he or she is. If you're not in for the long haul, then hit the road.

Work

They make excellent actors, detectives, spies, even teachers. There's just no telling where all that rawness of perception can take a Scorpio.

Finances

Scorpios are masters at using other people's money to build their own fortunes. This is as true of a Mafia don as it is of a

Wall Street entrepreneur. Scorpio attaches no moral judgment to it; this is simply how things are. In return, Scorpios can be extravagantly generous in charity work or anonymous donations to worthy causes. Your Scorpio may even rewrite the last act of your rejected screenplay and get it to sell big time.

Physical Scorpio

All Scorpios seem to share the same compelling, intense eyes. Regardless of body height or size, they generate a powerful sense of presence and usually have low, husky voices. Due to the unusual will power inherent in the sign, Scorpios often work to the point of exhaustion. Any illness usually has a strong emotional component.

Spirituality

Some Scorpios take to organized religion like a duck to water. They like the ritual and the sense of belonging. Others, however, delve into unorthodox belief systems seeking spiritual answers. Whatever form spirituality takes for a Scorpio, he or she brings passion and sincerity to the search.

Notable Scorpio People

Howard Baker
Fanny Brice
Prince Charles
Michael Crichton
Richard Dreyfuss
Linda Evans
Sally Field
Goldie Hawn
Katherine Hepburn

Billie Jean King
Timothy Leary
Pablo Picasso
George Patton
Carl Sagan
Jonas Salk
Martin Scorsese
Jaclyn Smith
Marlo Thomas

Sagittarius ↗

THE ARCHER (NOVEMBER 22–DECEMBER 21)

Element: Fire

Quality: Mutable

Keyword: Idealism, freedom

Planetary Ruler: Jupiter

Rules: Hips, thighs, liver, and hepatic system; natural ruler of the ninth house

These people seek the truth, express it as they see it, and don't care if no one else agrees with them. They see the large picture of any issue and can't be bothered with the mundane details. They are always outspoken and can't understand why other people aren't as candid. After all, what's there to hide?

This is a mentally oriented sign where logic reigns supreme. But the mentality differs from Gemini, the polar opposite of

Sagittarius, in several important ways. A Gemini is concerned with the here and now; he needs to know how and why things and relationships work in his life. A Sagittarian, however, focuses on the future and on the larger family of humanity. Quite often, this larger family includes animals—large, small, wild, or domestic—and the belief that all deserve the right to live free.

Despite the Sagittarian's propensity for logic, they are often quite prescient, with an uncanny ability to glimpse the future. Even when they have this ability, however, they often think they need an external tool to trigger it such as tarot cards, an astrology chart, or runes.

They love their freedom and chafe at any restrictions. Their versatility and natural optimism win them many friends, but only a few ever really know the heart of the Sagittarian.

Sagittarius Woman

She's hard to figure at first. You see her in a crowd and notice that she commands attention. She's humorous, vivacious, outspoken. One to one, she's flirtatious. But the moment you mention having dinner or catching a movie, she's gone. It's not that she's coy; it's simply that you're just a face in the crowd.

If you catch her attention, however, it's because you talk well and quickly about something that interests her. Animal rights, for instance, or paradigm shifts in worldwide belief systems. The lady thinks big and if you want to win her heart, you'd better think just as big.

Sagittarian women excel in jobs and careers that don't confine them. If they have children, they allow their offspring such great latitude that to other people it may appear that they're indifferent. This is hardly the case. A Sagittarian mother is loving and devoted, but believes that her children should find their own way. She offers broad guidelines and her own wisdom but doesn't force her opinions.

Sagittarius Man

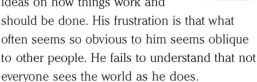

He's a charmer, flirtatious and witty, the kind of man everyone loves to have at a party. He's also candid and opinionated, with firm ideas on how things work and should be done. His frustration is that what often seems so obvious to him seems oblique to other people. He fails to understand that not everyone sees the world as he does.

His vision is broad and often grandiose. He does everything in a big way and is rarely satisfied with what he achieves. On his way to attaining a particular goal, he gets carried away with the momentum he has built up and ends up taking on more than he can handle.

He enjoys traveling, particularly foreign travel, and is too restless for a sedentary lifestyle. During his free time, this man is out horseback riding, practicing archery, or maybe whitewater rafting. He's always moving and aiming toward the future.

The less evolved men of this sign sometimes lose sight of the difference between need and greed. They want everything and they want it immediately. This is as true in business as it is in romance. Sagittarian men often have more than one relationship going on at a time, which suits their need for freedom. For this reason, Sagittarius is also known as the bachelor sign.

Sagittarius Kids

From the time they are old enough to have friends, your phone will never stop ringing. Sagittarius kids possess an optimism and vivaciousness that makes other kids feel good about themselves. A Sagittarius kid is always the center of attention. Their candor may be welcome with friends but not with adults in their life. A Sagittarius child may refuse to surrender his or her opinion to anyone.

As a parent of a Sagittarian child, your best approach is to establish the parameters of authority early. Always allow her the freedom to say what she thinks and believes, even if you don't agree. The Sagittarian child needs to know she won't be reprimanded for standing up for what she believes.

Compatibility

Other fire and air signs are compatible with Sagittarius. The Sagittarius-Gemini polarity confers a natural affinity between the two signs.

Remember the movie *Two for the Road* with Audrey Hepburn and Albert Finney? The romance between Hepburn and Finney definitely fell under a Sagittarian influence. The exotic place, their individual searches for truth, and the truths they ultimately found in each other are Sagittarian themes. No matter who a Sagittarian loves or marries, a part of him or her is always slightly separate and singular, aware of the larger picture.

Work

Constraint isn't in the Sagittarian vocabulary. Or if it is, the word and the reality influence other people's lives, not the Sagittarian's. They work best in jobs and fields where they have complete freedom to call the shots: an owner of an airline, CEO, small business owner, entrepreneur, actor, writer, or traveling salesman. The point isn't the work so much as the freedom of the work. That is always the bottom line with Sagittarius.

Finances

A Sagittarius has plenty of options about where to spend his or her money—travel, education, workshops, seminars, animals, or books—and that's often the problem. How can they narrow their choices? What should they buy first? More than likely they will toss all their choices into the air and seize the one that hits ground first.

Physical Sagittarius

Many people born under this sign are tall and wide through the shoulders. They may have a tendency to gain weight because they indulge their appetites. Jupiter, the planet of expansion, rules this sign and often expands the physical body as well. The face tends to be oval and elongated.

Spirituality

As the natural ruler of the ninth house, which governs philosophy, religion, and higher education, Sagittarians generally sample a vast array of spiritual beliefs. Once they find a belief system that suits them, they generally stick with it. In this way they are much like their polar opposites, Gemini. The difference, though, is that Sagittarius delves very deeply.

Notable Sagittarius People

Woody Allen
Jeff Bridges
Dale Carnegie
Emily Dickinson
Walt Disney
Jane Fonda
Betty Grable
Jimi Hendrix
Chet Huntley

Don Johnson
Caroline Kennedy
Brenda Lee
Mary Martin
Margaret Mead
Agnes Moorehead
Nostradamus
Frank Sinatra
Dionne Warwick

Capricorn ♑

THE GOAT (DECEMBER 22–JANUARY 19)

Element: Earth

Quality: Cardinal

Keyword: Materialism, self-discipline

Planetary Ruler: Saturn

Rules: Knees, skin, and bones; natural ruler of the tenth house

Capricorns are serious-minded people who often seem aloof and tightly in control of their emotions and their personal domain. Even as youngsters, there's a mature air about them, as if they were born with a profound core that few outsiders ever see.

This sign's nickname, the goat, represents Capricorn's slow, steady rise through the world. They're easily impressed by outward signs of success, but are interested less in money than in the power that money represents. Like Scorpio, they feel the need to rule whatever kingdom they occupy whether it's their home, work place, or business. Like Scorpios, they prize power and mastery over others, but they tend to be more subtle about it.

Capricorns are true workers—industrious, efficient, and disciplined. They deplore inertia in other people. Their innate common sense gives them the ability to plan ahead and to work out practical ways of approaching goals. More often than not, they succeed at whatever they set out to do.

In a crowd, Capricorns aren't particularly easy to spot. They aren't physically distinctive the way Scorpios are, and they aren't the life of the party like Sagittarians. But they possess a quiet dignity that's unmistakable.

Capricorns are natural worriers. Even when they've done their homework and taken all precautions they can possibly take, they fret that they've forgotten something. They benefit from

the cultivation of "perfect faith" that whatever
they do will work out fine.

Capricorn Woman

At first glance, she appears to
be tough as nails, a determined,
serious woman who seems to
know where she has been, where she is, and
where she's going. But when you get to know
her, you discover she's not tough at all; she's
merely guarded and reserved. Don't expect her
to welcome you into her life with open arms.
You have to prove yourself first.

This woman has certain parameters and
boundaries that she simply won't cross. She
isn't the type to throw herself recklessly into a
casual affair. Once you've proven you're worth
her while, she opens up emotionally and her
depth may astonish you. She plays for keeps
in love.

As a mother, she's devoted and often runs her home with the efficiency of a business. Due to the Saturn influence on this sign, the Capricorn woman can sometimes be too rigid with her spouse and children. She expects a lot and, supported by other aspects in her chart, may enforce her will to the point of dominance. She has a soft spot for animals, which often bring out the best in her simply because she opens to them emotionally.

Capricorn Man

He's well prepared for any journey he undertakes and it doesn't matter whether the journey is physical, emotional, or spiritual. He doesn't like surprises. He shies away from getting involved in people's lives and this detachment him allows him to focus on his goals. As a boss, he can be dictatorial, ordering people around with absolute impunity. As an employee, you won't find a harder worker.

He enjoys the company of vivacious women, perhaps because they make him feel lighter and less driven. Once he's committed, he tends to be monogamous. Life seems to improve for him as he ages, perhaps because he has learned that discipline is not nearly as important as compassion.

Capricorn Kids

Capricorn children can converse as easily with other kids as they can with adults. They are at ease with adults and, in some respects, actually consider them equals. This doesn't mean that they never act like kids. When they loosen up, they can be wild and unpredictable, but probably never reckless.

Like their adult counterparts, Capricorn children attack whatever they do with efficiency and patience. They often exhibit deep compassion for people less fortunate. As the parent of a Capricorn child, teach him or her to lighten up!

As a parent, he is similar to the Capricorn mother's emphasis on rules, and parameters.

Compatibility

Virgos may be too mental and picky and Taureans too fixed, but because they have the earth element in common, they get along with Capricorns. Of the water signs, the intensity of Scorpios may be overwhelming and the ambivalence of Pisces may drive them nuts. Capricorns get along well with Cancers because both are cardinal signs.

Romance

At times, Capricorns need a partner who is serious, while other

times they need the comic, the lighthearted inno-
cent who makes them laugh. Which mate they
end up with depends on where they are in life.
That may be true for all of us to one extent or
another, but it's especially true for the Capricorn.

Ultimately, the Capricorn's path is always
serious business. No matter how hard you make
them laugh, their path always leads back to the
same riddle. Regardless of how hard they work,
how far they climb, or how emotionally or physically rich they become, it's never enough. It
only leads back to the solitude of self.

Work

Capricorns excel in any profession that is
structured, such as engineering, medicine,
editing, politics, ceramics, building,
architecture, and leatherwork. Their
strong desire to succeed is colored
by traditional values and a conservative

approach. In some Capricorns, these traits make them exceptionally good workers who progress slowly and successfully toward their goals. With other Capricorns, the tradition and conservatism hold them back.

Finances

Thriftiness is the hallmark for Capricorn finances. They build their finances the same way they build their careers, one penny at a time. They do seek status and the acquisition of material goods that reflect what they seek, so they go through periods where they overspend.

Physical Capricorn

They aren't the body-builder types. But because they are earth signs, they generally appreciate the benefits of exercise and have

something physical that they do regularly. Their knees tend to trouble them. Because the sign is sometimes repressed emotionally, Capricorns benefit by venting what they feel, which in turn improves their physical bodies.

Spirituality

Capricorns flourish within structured and firmly established parameters. Ritual speaks to them and inspires them. They bring the same serious efficiency to their involvement with spiritual beliefs as they do to other areas of their lives. In less evolved types, the expression of spiritual beliefs can manifest as dogma. In the highly evolved Capricorn, the soul clearly understands its purpose in this life.

Notable Capricorn People

Humphrey Bogart

David Bowie

E. L. Doctorow

Faye Dunaway

Jose Ferrer

Cary Grant

J. Edgar Hoover

William James

James Earl Jones

Diane Keaton

Martin Luther King, Jr.

Mary Tyler Moore

Sir Isaac Newton

Dolly Parton

Edgar Allen Poe

Elvis Presley

J.D. Salinger

Albert Schweitzer

Josef Stalin

Aquarius ♒

WATER BEARER (JANUARY 20–FEBRUARY 18)

Element: Air

Quality: Fixed

Planetary Ruler: Uranus

Keyword: Altruism, individuality, freedom

Rules: Ankles, shins, and circulatory system; natural ruler of the eleventh house

Aquarians are original thinkers, often eccentric, who prize individuality and freedom above all else. The tribal mentality goes against their grain. They chafe at the restrictions placed upon them by society and seek to follow their own paths.

Aquarius is the sign of true genius because these people generally have the ability to think in unique ways. Once they make up their minds about something, nothing can convince them to change what they believe. This stubbornness is a double-edged sword; it can sustain them or destroy them. When the stubbornness manifests in small rebellions against the strictures of society, energy is wasted that could be put to better use.

Even though compassion is a hallmark of this sun sign, Aquarians usually don't become emotionally involved with the causes they promote. Their compassion, while genuine, rises from the intellect rather than the heart. The Uranian influence confers a fascination with a broad spectrum of intellectual interests.

Aquarius Woman

Even when you know her well, she's hard to figure because she's so often a bundle of paradoxes. She's patient but impatient; a nonconformist who conforms when it suits her;

rebellious but peace-loving; stubborn and yet compliant when she wants to be.

She likes unusual people and has a variety of friends, both male and female. Economic status doesn't impress her, so her friends tend to come from a broad spectrum of backgrounds. Like the people she associates with, the Aquarian woman has many interests. She may dabble in tarot or astrology, have a passion for invention or writing, or may be a budding filmmaker. Whatever her profession, it allows her latitude to do things her way.

In romance, the only given with this woman is that she's attracted to someone who is unusual or eccentric in some way. Even if the significant other appears to be conventional, he isn't. As a mother, she allows her children the freedom to make their own decisions, revels in their accomplishments, and never lets them down.

Aquarius Man

He's often as inscrutable as his female counterpart and for the same reasons. He wants companionship, but not at the expense of his individuality. Even when he marries, he retains his independence to often irritating extremes. He might, for instance, fly off to some exotic place, leaving his wife or significant other to tend to his affairs at home.

The Aquarian man is fascinated by unusual people and places. Even though his attention is focused on the future, he may be interested in the mysteries of ancient cultures—how the pyramids were built, the true nature of Stonehenge, or the disappearance of the Anasazi. His travel to foreign cultures is often connected to these interests.

Aquarian men and women are both natural revolutionaries. If the restrictions placed on them are too confining, they rebel in a major way. But both need a place to which they can return, a sanctuary where they can refresh themselves. When the Aquarian man returns from his exotic journeys, he's eager to indulge himself in his family. As a parent, he may seem remote at times and perhaps somewhat undemonstrative, but his love for his offspring runs deep.

Aquarius Kids

They don't recognize barriers of any kind among people, so their friends span the gamut of the social and economic spectrum. They tend to be extroverts, but can also be content in solitary pursuits, their little minds busy with the stuff of the universe. They can be as stubborn as a Taurus, particularly when it comes to defending something they believe in.

Even though these kids get along well with their peers, they aren't followers. They aren't afraid to disagree with the consensus opinion. Within a family structure, they need to know they have the freedom to speak their own minds and that their opinions are heard. They may chafe at rules that are too rigid and strict.

Compatibility

Due to the lack of prejudice in this sign, Aquarians usually get along with just about everyone. They're particularly attracted to people with whom they share an intellectual camaraderie. A sign that's sextile or trine to Aquarius is usually very compatible as is Aquarius's polar opposite, Leo.

Romance

Aquarians need the same space and freedom in a relationship that they crave in every other area of their lives. Even when they commit, the need doesn't evaporate. They must follow the dictates of their individuality above all else. This stubbornness can work against them if they aren't careful. Aquarians usually are attracted to people who are unusual or eccentric in some way. Their most intimate relationships are marked by uniqueness.

Work

They work best in avant garde fields: film, the arts, cutting-edge research in electronics, computers, or psychology. Many have raw psychic talent that can be developed into clairvoyance, remote viewing, and precognition, and most are very intuitive. The main element they seek in their work is freedom.

Finances

Aquarians are generous with their families and loved ones and that compassion extends to the larger scope of humanity as well. They stash money away, but the accumulation of wealth isn't the point; their freedom is.

Physical Aquarius

The typical Aquarian is usually tall and slender with a complexion that is lighter than his or her ethnic group. With Uranus ruling the sign, Aquarians have a sensitive nervous system and can be easily excitable. They should guard against exhausting their energy reserves; their minds are incessantly busy.

Spirituality

The revolutionary nature of the sign definitely extends to spiritual issues. Even if an Aquarian is born into a family that follows the dictates of an organized religion, he or she probably won't stick to it. Aquarians insist on finding their own path and seek a broader spiritual spectrum that honors "the family of man."

Notable Aquarius People

Alan Alda

Tom Brokaw

Natalie Cole

James Cromwell

Christian Dior

Farrah Fawcett

Zsa Zsa Gabor

Gene Hackman

Charles Lindbergh

James Michener

Graham Nash

Paul Newman

Burt Reynolds

Tom Selleck

Emmanuel Swedenborg

John Travolta

Pisces ♓

THE FISH (FEBRUARY 19–MARCH 20)

Element: Water

Quality: Mutable

Keyword: Compassion, mysticism

Planetary Ruler: Neptune

Rules: The feet and is associated with the lymphatic system; natural ruler of the twelfth house

Pisces need to explore their world through their emotions. They feel things so deeply that quite often they become a kind of psychic sponge, absorbing the emotions of people around them. Because of this, they should choose their friends and associates carefully.

People born under this sign usually have wonderful imaginations and great creative resources. They gravitate toward the arts in general and to theater and film in particular.

In the business world, they tend to make powerful administrators and managers because they are so attuned to the thoughts of the people around them.

Pisces people need time alone so that they can detach from the emotions of people around them and center themselves. Without periodic solitude, it becomes increasingly difficult for them to sort out what they feel from what other people feel. They are very impressionable. They also tend to be moody because they feel the very height of joy and the utter depths of despair.

Love and romance are essential for most Piscean individuals. It fulfills them emotionally and they generally flourish within stable relationships.

Pisces, represented by the fish swimming in opposite directions, can be ambivalent and indecisive simply because they're so impressionable. In highly evolved types, mystical tendencies are

well developed and the individuals possess
deeply spiritual connections.

Pisces Woman

She's mysterious, with an air of
complexity about her, as if she knows
more than she's telling. Her eyes are
large, gentle, and almost liquid with
compassion. The lady is all feeling
and possesses a quiet strength that
hints at inner depths.

Don't ever be dogmatic with her. She
refuses to be limited or restricted by anyone or
anything that might inhibit her freedom of
expression. This is reflected in her job, her
home, and her relationship with her family and
friends. This tendency may sometimes work
against her, but she doesn't care. It's against
her nature to be otherwise.

Even though she needs companionship, she
also craves her solitude. It's as essential to her

well-being as harmony is to a Libra. When she doesn't have her time alone, she may be prone to alcohol or drug abuse. Properly channeled, her energy can produce astonishing works in art, literature, and music. In this instance, she becomes a mystical channel for the higher mind.

As a mother, her psychic connection to her children allows her to understand what they're feeling even when they don't understand it themselves.

Pisces Man

His quiet strength and self-containment fascinate women. He's a good listener, the kind of man who gives you his full attention when you're talking. He's also a fine friend to people he trusts, always there when his friends are in need. But, like his female counterpart, he's a sucker for a sob story; he can't stand seeing tragedies or heartbreaks in others.

In affairs of the heart, the Pisces man is a true romantic, even if he doesn't want to admit it to himself. He likes candlelight dinners and intimate conversation. It may take him a while to fall head over heels in love, but once he does, his emotions run deep and eternal.

The Pisces man may gravitate toward the arts or, because the sign rules the twelfth house, may work behind the scene in some capacity. Whatever his path, he needs to learn to balance the demands of his inner life with his responsibilities in the external world.

Pisces Kids

In a crowd, the easiest way to pick out a Pisces child is by the  liquid eyes. Their gaze seems wise, ancient, as if they have seen worlds the rest of us haven't even imagined. Pisces kids tend to have vivid dreams and many of them manifest an early interest in psychic phenomena. If the mystical tendencies are nurtured and encouraged, a Pisces child can grow into a true medium, clairvoyant, or healer.

These kids feel everything with such intensity that a cross look is probably all a parent needs to keep them in line. If you raise your voice to a Pisces child, it's the equivalent of a physical assault. Their feelings are easily hurt.

Compatibility

Other water signs seem the obvious choice here. But Scorpio might overpower Pisces and Cancer might be too clinging. The signs sextile to Pisces are Capricorn and Taurus. While Capricorn might be too limited and grounded for the Piscean imagination, Taurus probably fits right in. Gemini, because it's a mutable sign like Pisces, can also be compatible.

Romance

Through the heart, sensitive
Pisces experiences his subjective
reality as real, solid, perhaps even
more tangible than the external world.
For some Pisces, romance can be the
point of transcendence, the source where he
penetrates to the larger mysteries that have concerned him most of his life. To be romantically
involved with a Pisces is to be introduced to
many levels of consciousness and awareness. If
you're not up to it, then get out now because
your Pisces isn't going to change.

Work

Pisces do well in anything
that is behind the scenes. Due to
their dreamy imaginations and mys-
tical leanings, they excel in the arts, literature,
and drama, or as monks, mystics, even inven-
tors. Piscean Edgar Cayce, the "sleeping

prophet," is probably the best example of what a Pisces is capable of doing in metaphysics. Piscean Albert Einstein is one of the best examples of Pisces as scientific genius.

Finances

Pisces is usually less concerned about money and material goods than he is about enjoying what he does to make a living. Can he transcend himself through his work? Does his tremendous compassion find expression through his work? If not, then he will undoubtedly change his work again and again, until he finds the job or profession that suits him.

Physical Pisces

There are two types of Pisces individuals—the whale and the dolphin. The first tends to be physically large— in height and in weight. The second tends to be smaller, more graceful.

The whale often looks awkward when he walks, as if his feet are too small for the rest of him. His dolphin counterpart is, in contrast, like a dancer, at home in his body. The extraordinary eyes that are typical of the Pisces individual are exemplified in the violet eyes of Elizabeth Taylor.

Since Pisces rules the feet, most individuals with a Pisces Sun, Moon, or Ascendant benefit from foot massage and foot reflexology.

Spirituality

Not all Pisces people are psychic, of course, or mystically inclined. Not all of them want to become monks or nuns, either. But most Pisces people are born with a deep intuitive sense, even if it's latent. And this sense is what connects them to a higher power. It may manifest within the parameters of organized religion—or it may veer into something less structured. Whatever form it takes, the intuitive side of Pisces seeks expression.

Notable Pisces People

Michael Caine	Rex Harrison
Frederic Chopin	Ron Howard
Albert Einstein	Andrew Jackson
Mikhail Gorbachev	Jerry Lewis
Peter Graves	Liza Minnelli
Jean Harlow	B.F. Skinner
George Harrison	Elizabeth Taylor

Princess Diana and Astrology

Within hours of Princess Di's death in Paris on
August 31, 1997, the astrology boards on the
web literally hummed. Her birth chart and transits to her chart went up like billboards along
the information highway. Every astrologer had
an opinion about the celestial movements that
had caused the accident.

Some astrologers focused on aspects that
clearly indicated that alcohol or drug abuse had
been involved. Other astrologers pinpointed
aspects that spoke tomes about her relationship
with the royal family. Some speculated that a
conspiracy might be behind it because of her
relationship with Dodi al Fayed.

In *The Mountain Astrologer,* an eminent
magazine in the astrology field, one astrologer
wrote: "At her death, transiting Neptune exactly
conjoined her Saturn, while Uranus conjoined
Jupiter, the ruler of her chart. Neptune dissolved

the structure and Uranus, as shocking as it was, set her free."

To an astrologer, this language is eloquent; it precisely describes celestial movements that affected physical life. But what, exactly, do the words mean?

In yet another article about Diana's death, an astrologer notes that Diana's natal Venus was conjunct Caput Algol, the fixed star at 25 degrees Taurus. This star is known as "the evil one" and is associated with violent death. In Diana's chart, it is placed in her fifth house of children. At the very least, this would suggest her children might be taken from her through divorce. But, as Dawne Kovan wrote, "The tragic reality is that it is she who has been taken from them."

Kovan goes on to explore the prominent role that eclipses played in Diana's life. Her marriage to Prince Charles occurred within two days of a solar eclipse; Prince William was born during an eclipse; Diana's separation from the prince was announced on a lunar eclipse; and she died less than twenty-four hours before a solar eclipse on September 1, 1997.

All of this is as fascinating as Diana's life. But the bottom line is that death in a chart is fairly easy to spot after the fact and nearly impossible to predict before the fact. Astrologer Grant Lewi allegedly predicted his own death, but we don't know whether that was astrology speaking or the voice of his own intuition.

What might Princess Diana's astrologer have said to her? At best, she might have warned the princess that certain patterns would be taking shape that might endanger her. She might have warned the princess to be careful on the highway, to stay clear of any driver who had been drinking. She might have advised her to stay put between certain dates. But for the most part, these kinds of warnings are common sense. It's doubtful that Diana's astrologer told her she might die around the time of the solar eclipse on September 1, 1997. Doubtful because most contemporary astrologers realize that an individual's free will governs the blueprint of the birth chart.

CHAPTER 2

The Planets, Astrology, and You

Astrology and Intuition

When I was eight or nine, one of my uncles took me, my sister, and several cousins on an adventure I've never forgotten. It took place in his back yard in Oklahoma, on a clear summer night, when each of us got a turn to peer through the magical lens of his new telescope.

That night, I saw the rings of Saturn, the red dust of Mars, the stark landscape of the

moon. And suddenly, the stories about the
Greek and Roman gods that my mother read
to me leaped to life. The outer evidence
fused with an inner certainty, intellect joined
intuition, pieces slammed together. In a
moment of utter clarity, I understood why
Mars was the god of war, why Mercury was
the messenger, why Neptune ruled the seas
and everything beneath them. I intuitively
sensed connections.

Planets are the expression of energy. They
are classified as benefic or malefic, good
or bad. These terms are misleading since planetary energy
isn't positive or energy; our use
of the energy determines
whether it's positive or negative. Traditionally, Jupiter is
the great benefic, the

planet that blesses. Venus comes in a close second. The Sun, Moon, and Mercury line up after that. Saturn is the great malefic, the big bad guy of the group whose lessons tend to be harsh. He's followed by Mars, Uranus, Neptune, and Pluto.

Inner and Outer Planets

Planets orbit the sun at different speeds. The closer a planet is to the sun, the faster it travels through its orbit. The Moon, for instance, travels through the zodiac in about 28 days and spends 2 to 3 days in each sign. Mercury orbits the Sun in 88 days. Pluto, which lies the farthest from the sun, completes its orbit in 248 years. The faster moving planets—Moon, Mercury, Venus, Mars—are known as inner planets. Jupiter, Uranus,

Neptune, and Pluto are known as outer planets.

The inner planets are considered to be personal because they relate to the development of our individual egos, our conscious selves. The outer planets relate to the outer world. Since the outer planets move so much more slowly through the zodiac, their pattern of influence is often felt by an entire generation of people.

The luminaries—Sun and Moon—also have transpersonal qualities. The Sun represents not only our ego, but fundamental cosmic energy. The Moon, which concerns our most intimate emotions and urges, links us to what astrologer Robert Hand calls, "One's Ultimate Source."

Planetary Motion

Planetary motion is either direct (D), retrograde (R), or stationary (S). In reality, all planetary motion is direct but relative motion isn't.

The Sun and the Moon can never turn retrograde, but all of the other planets do. A retrograde planet is one that appears to move backward in the zodiac, but this backward motion is actually an optical illusion. Imagine being in a train as another train speeds past you. You feel as if you're moving backward, when in actuality you're only moving more slowly than the other train. Retrograde motion doesn't change the fundamental essence of a planet; it merely means that the expression of its energy is altered somewhat.

Earth

During a Mercury retrograde, for instance, communications tend to get fouled up and travel plans are disrupted. During a Jupiter retrograde, the beneficial aspects of the planet are turned down somewhat. Some astrologers contend that if there are three or more retrograde planets in a chart, certain past life patterns may prevail in the present life. But even if it is true, our point of power lies in the present, in this life, this moment.

During a retrograde, the nature of that planet is forced inward, where it creates tension and stress. The outlet for this tension is usually worked out in relationships with others.

Planets in direct motion have more influence than retrograde planets. Stationary planets, those that are about to turn direct or retrograde, have greater influence in a chart than either retrograde or direct moving planets. This is due to the concentrated energy of the planet.

The Planets

The Sun: Your Ego ☉

Think beach, blue skies, sunlight spilling across the white sand. The Sun is the very essence and energy of life, the manifestation of will, power, and desire. It represents the ego, individuality, the yang principle and is the thrust that allows us to meet challenges and expand our lives. The Sun represents a person's creative abilities and the general state of his or her physical health.

The Sun embraces the fatherhood principle and in a chart, symbolizes a person's natural father and a woman's husband. As natural ruler of the fifth house, it rules children in general and the firstborn in particular. Since the Sun also symbolizes authority and power, a strongly placed Sun confers leadership ability. A Sun that is badly aspected or which is weakly placed lessens the natural vitality and may make it difficult for the person to express basic drives and desires.

The Sun spends about a month in each sign, with a mean daily motion of 59'8". It rules occupations of power and authority—royalty and religious and spiritual rulers. Its natural house is the fifth and it governs the sign of Leo. It rules the heart, back, spine, and spinal cord.

The Moon: Your Emotions ☾

The inner you. Intuition. The feminine. The mother. The yin principle. Coupled with the Sun and the Ascendant, the Moon is one of the vital parts of a chart. It describes our emotional reactions to situations, how emotions flow through us, motivating and compelling us—or limiting us and holding us back.

The Moon symbolizes a person's mother and the relationship between mother and child.

In a man's chart, the Moon represents his wife; in a woman's chart, it describes pregnancies, childbirth, and intuition. Symbolically, the Moon represents our capacity to become part of the whole rather than attempting to master the parts. It asks that we become whatever it is that we seek.

As Earth's satellite, the Moon moves more swiftly than any of the planets, completing a circuit of the zodiac in less than 28 days. It rules activities and professions dealing with children and those that concern the sea. Its natural house is the fourth and it governs the sign of Cancer. The stomach, breasts, mammary glands, womb, conception, and the body fluids in general are ruled by the Moon.

Mercury: Your Intellect ☿

Mental quickness. Verbal acuity. Communication. Our mental picture of the world. Mercury is the messenger; it speaks in terms of logic and reasoning. The left brain is its vehicle. Mercury represents how we think and how we communicate those thoughts. Mercury also is concerned with travel of the routine variety—work commutes, trips across town, weekend excursions, or a visit with siblings and neighbors—rather than long distance travel.

Restlessness is inherent to Mercury because it craves movement, newness, and the bright hope of undiscovered terrains. Mercury often tackles something new before the old has been assimilated. On a higher level, Mercury seeks to understand the deeper connections between the physical universe and the divine.

Mercury orbits the Sun in about 88 days. It goes retrograde every few months and during that time communications and travel plans go haywire. Your computer may go down, lightning may blow out your electricity, or you may spend hours in an airport waiting for a flight that is ultimately canceled. It's best not to sign contracts when Mercury is retrograde.

Mercury

Mercury rules any profession dealing with writing, teaching, speaking, books, and publications. Mercury is the natural ruler of the third and sixth houses and governs Gemini and Virgo. It rules arms, hands, shoulders, lungs, the solar plexus, abdomen, intestines, the thymus gland, and the nervous and respiratory systems.

Venus: Your Love Life ♀

Romance. Beauty. Artistic instinct. Sociability. Venus governs our ability to attract compatible people, to create close personal relationships and to form business partnerships. It expresses how we relate to other people one-on-one and how we express ourselves in marriage and in romantic relationships.

Since Venus determines our spontaneous attractions to other people, it's one of the areas to look at when doing chart comparisons for compatibility. When Venus falls in another person's Sun sign, it enhances the initial attraction and bodes well for overall compatibility. This planet, along with the Moon, is associated with maternal love in that it gives what it has freely and without strings attached.

Venus

Venus is associated with the arts and the aesthetic sense, and it has enormous influence on our tastes in art, music, and literature. The sign and placement of Venus, as well as its aspects, determine our refinement—or lack of it. This planet also has some bearing on material resources, earning capacity, and spending habits. A strong Venus enhances these things; a poorly placed or badly aspected Venus generates laziness, self-indulgence, extravagance, and discord in partnerships.

Venus orbits the Sun in 255 days. It spends about four weeks in a sign when moving direct and is retrograde for about six weeks. It rules all professions having to do with the arts and music. Its natural houses are the second and the seventh, and it governs Taurus and Libra. It rules the neck, throat, thyroid gland, kidneys, ovaries, veins, and circulation of the venous blood. It shares rulership with the Moon over the female sex organs.

Mars: Your Energy ♂

Dynamic expression. Aggression. Individualism. Sexual drive. Action. Mars dictates our survival energy and the shape that energy assumes as we define ourselves in terms of the larger world. It represents the individualization process, particularly in a romantic relationship. A weak Mars placement in a woman's chart may make her too passive and submissive in a love relationship, especially if her significant other has a strongly placed Mars.

Mars rules athletes and competitions. The true Mars individual seeks to take himself to the limit—and then sur-pass that limit. He refuses to compro-mise his integrity by following another's agenda. He doesn't compare himself to other people and doesn't want to dominate or be dominated. He simply wants to be free to follow his own path, whatever it is.

Mars

Mars' energy can be either constructive or destructive; it depends on how it's channeled. Rage, violence, and brutality can manifest if the energy is poorly channeled. When properly channeled, Mars' energy manifests as stamina and achievement.

Mars orbits the sun in 687 days. It spends six to eight weeks in a sign. When retrograde, it sits in a sign for two and half months.

As the god of war, Mars governs the military, rules Aries, and is co-ruler of Scorpio. Its natural houses are the first and the eighth. It rules the head, general musculature of the body, the sex organs in general—the male sex organs in particular—the anus, red corpuscles, and hemoglobin.

Jupiter: Your Higher Mind ♃

Philosophy. Religion. Higher education. Expansion and integration. Growth. Tradition views Jupiter as the great benefic planet, associated with luck, success, achievement, and prosperity. But it can also indicate excess, laziness, and other less desirable traits. The bottom line, though, is that Jupiter's energies are usually constructive.

This planet's energy is what allows us to reach out beyond ourselves and expand our consciousness. It confers a love of travel and a need to explore religious and philosophical ideas. Jupiter also allows us to

Jupiter

integrate ourselves into the larger social order—church or religion, community, and corporation.

Since Jupiter rules the abstract mind, it describes our intellectual and spiritual interests in the most profound sense. In terms of the body, Jupiter can often lead to a physical expansion as well: weight gain.

Jupiter takes about twelve years to traverse the zodiac and averages a year in every sign. It governs publishing, the travel profession, universities and other institutions of higher learning, and traditional organized religions. Its natural houses are the ninth and the twelfth. It rules Sagittarius. Jupiter oversees the blood in general, arteries, hips, thighs, and feet (with Neptune).

Saturn: Your Responsibilities, Karma ♄

Discipline. Responsibility. Limitations and restrictions. Obedience. Building of foundations. No free rides. Saturn has long been known as the great malefic. While it's true that its lessons are sometimes harsh, it also provides structure and foundation, and teaches us through experience what we need in order to grow. It shows us the limitations we have and teaches us the rules of the game in this physical reality.

Astrologer Jean Avery, writing in *Astrology and Your Past Lives,* says: "The description of Saturn's placement, aspects, and rulerships in the horoscope is most important in the process of uncovering past life experiences." Even if you don't believe in reincarnation, there's ample evidence that

Saturn holds a key to what the soul intends to accomplish in this life.

People with a well placed or well aspected Saturn tend to have a practical, prudent outlook. When poorly aspected, Saturn creates rigid belief systems, restricts growth, and closes us off to other possibilities. A delicate balance must be grasped about Saturn influences. Even though it pushes us to understand and work with limitations, it can also cause us to settle for too little, to deny our creative expression because we don't want to see what is really possible.

As one of the outer, slowly moving planets, Saturn takes twenty-nine and a half years to cross the zodiac. Its natural houses are the tenth and the eleventh. It rules

Saturn

Capricorn. This planet governs the bones and joints, skin, and teeth.

Uranus: Your Individuality ♅

Sudden, unexpected disruptions. Breaks with tradition and old patterns to make room for the new. Genius. Eccentricity. Astrologer Steven Forrest considers Uranus the ruler of astrology; Robert Hand calls Uranus, Neptune, and Pluto "transcendental planets" that can be dealt with constructively only with an expanded consciousness. Unless we nurture a larger perspective, Uranian disruptions appear to bring unpleasant and unexpected surprises. In reality, these disruptions liberate us, revolutionize the way we do things, and blow out the old so that the new can flow in.

Uranus

Uranus, like the other outer planets, remains in a sign for so long that its effect is felt on the masses. Today, at the start of the twenty-first century, this planet's influence is visible in the breakdown of old paradigms of belief within most of the large structures we have taken for granted: health care, medicine, science, religion, lifestyle, education, social programs. We stand at the brink of a new century with old structures crumbling around us. But in the shadows, the new paradigms are forming, bubbling with vitality, gathering momentum. This is all part of the Uranian influence.

In a horoscope, Uranus dictates the areas of our life in which these disruptions occur and how we utilize this energy. Do we feel it? Think about it? Seize it?

Pull it deep within us so that it becomes rooted in who we are? Are we so afraid of it that we deny it? Uranus also indicates the areas in which we are most inventive, creative, and original.

This planet takes 84 years to go through the zodiac. Its natural house is the eleventh and it rules Aquarius. Traditionally, before the discovery of Uranus in 1781, Saturn ruled this sign. But Saturn's rigidity just doesn't fit Aquarius. It governs electricity, inventions, the avant garde, everything that is unpredictable or sudden.

Neptune: Your Visionary Self ♆

Hidden. Psychic. Spiritual insights. Illusions. The unconscious. This planet stimulates the imagination, dreams, psychic experiences, artistic inspiration, flashes of insight, mystical tendencies. On the down side, it deals with all

forms of escapism—drug and alcohol addiction, as well as delusion.

Neptune, like Uranus, overpowers Saturn's rigidity. Where Uranus disrupts the rigidity, Neptune simply negates it. This planet is considered the higher octave of Venus, and when it operates in the chart of an evolved soul, its music is extraordinary. Edgar Cayce, known as the "sleeping prophet," was such an individual. While asleep, he was able to diagnose physical ailments for people he'd never met, using nothing more than their names.

Most of us experience Neptune through synchronous events and flashes of insight that seem to come out of nowhere. Or we lose ourselves in the illusions we've created. The best way to appreciate Neptune's energy is

Neptune

from a standpoint of quiet contemplation—meditation, yoga, listening to music, writing imaginative fiction, or through some activity that involves water.

As Steven Forrest writes in *The Inner Sky*, "Neptune asks us to go beyond the universe of ego, hunger, and aggression without sacrificing our ability to function as a personality."

Neptune takes 165 years to cross the zodiac and spends about 14 years in each sign. The twelfth house is its natural domain and it rules Pisces. It governs shipping, dance, film, and the arts in general, and is associated with mediums, clairvoyants, psychic healers, and both white and black magic.

Pluto: How You Transform and Regenerate Your Life ♀

Destiny. Transcendence. Redemption. Purge. Power. Afterlife. Good and evil. Pluto's influence is never ambivalent or passive. Although it sometimes works in subtle ways, its repercussion in our lives is far-reaching and transformational. Its two extremes are best symbolized by Hitler and Gandhi, each man possessed of a vision that he manifested in physical reality. Both had a mission, a sense of destiny, but one caused massive destruction and the other elevated mass consciousness.

In our personal lives, Pluto's influence is no different. Pluto tears down our habits and belief systems, the very structures that Saturn has helped us build, thus forcing us to transcend the ruin—or to smother in the debris.

Pluto

A Pluto placement in Sagittarius, in the ninth house of philosophy and spiritual beliefs, would mean you evolve through expansion of your beliefs in these areas. But before you do, Pluto will destroy your old beliefs, collapsing them like a house of cards.

Pluto, discovered in 1930, is the most distant planet from the Sun. It exists at the very edge of our solar system, its light so dim it seems almost etheric. It takes 248 years to com-

plete a circuit of the zodiac. Popular astrological theory says that Pluto, like Uranus and Neptune, wasn't discovered until humanity had evolved to the point to be able to understand its energy.

"Through it," writes Steven Forrest, "we

embody the visions and terrors of humanity. We represent them. We serve as a living symbol of some communal need or fear." Through Pluto, we tap into that which is larger than our individual selves. We tap into the collective mind in all its hypnotizing horror and magnificent beauty.

Since Pluto's discovery, its influence has been observed in only Cancer, Leo, Virgo, Libra, and Scorpio. In the late fall of 1995, Pluto slipped into Sagittarius. The transformation under this influence is apt to be enormous and far-reaching, completing the collapse of old paradigms and belief systems.

Pluto, the higher octave of Mars, governs various types of occult practices: black magic, levitation, witchcraft, and reincarnation. On a personal level in a horoscope, Pluto's influence is most powerful when it occupies a prominent place or rules the chart.

Key Words for the Planets

Sun: Vitality, ego, self-image.

Moon: Emotions, intuition, the yin.

Mercury: Culling and communication of information, mental quickness.

Venus: Love, romance, aesthetics, serenity.

Mars: Aggression, individuation, will.

Jupiter: Expansion, luck, higher mind.

Saturn: Discipline, limitations, building a solid foundation.

Uranus: Sudden and unexpected, disruption, genius, innovative.

Neptune: Illusion, inspiration, creative genius.

Pluto: Transformation, regeneration, the occult.

North Node: The point through which we break free of unconscious or past-life bias and evolve fully as spiritual beings.

South Node: The release of old, deeply embedded patterns we need to break.

Part of Fortune: A point of luck, success.

Intuition and Interpretation

Astrology is as much an art as it is a science. As with any art, the best impulses and ideas begin somewhere deep inside. They bubble up from the soup of the unconscious, make connections with the right brain, and suddenly leap into your conscious awareness as a flash of intuitive insight. These flashes of insight are invaluable when interpreting an astrology chart.

Several years ago, a friend asked me to interpret his birth chart as well as a progressed chart for the coming year. He recently had been laid off from his job at a computer company, his savings were nearly gone, and his relationship with the woman he'd been seeing for several years wasn't going well. His daughter from a previous marriage was rebelling against everything, and his ex-wife blamed him. To say he was at loose ends hardly covers the flux his life was in at the time.

After I interpreted his birth chart, I glanced at his progressed chart. I figured I would see more of the same problems, because this man is the kind who would rather avoid his problems than confront them. The first thing that struck me was Uranus transiting his fourth house of the home. I blurted that he was going to move suddenly and unexpectedly and that it wasn't just a move across town. I also said it would happen quickly and that he could possibly get married as well.

The man laughed and informed me he couldn't possibly move. He hardly had enough money to buy groceries. As for the marriage part, no way.

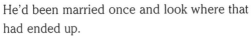

He'd been married once and look where that had ended up.

Six weeks later, this man was offered a job in Colorado. He sold everything he owned and moved out there. Not long after he arrived, he met a woman, fell in love, and they moved in together. For this man, the commitment to live with her was as good as a marriage.

Uranus transiting your natal fourth house doesn't have to mean a move. It may simply indicate sudden changes in your domestic life, a breaking away from your "roots." But to me, right then, it meant only one thing, a long distance, physical move from one place to another. The repercussions of the man's move, of course, followed the *overall* pattern for Uranus in the fourth house. It transformed his relationship with his family and girlfriend, broke him loose of childhood conditioning, and redefined his concept of security.

So when you have a birth chart in front of you, allow your intuition the freedom to make connections you might not perceive with your conscious mind. Sometimes, those connections are the only ones that matter to the other person. Don't allow the science part of astrology to become dogma. Learn the basics, assimilate them, then get out of the way so your intuition can speak to you.

The practice exercise that follows illustrates how intuition feels as you experience it. The sensation is different for everyone, but it does seem to register somewhere in the body while it's happening. It may be a tightening in your stomach, a sudden pulsing at your temple, or a flash of heat in your hands or fingertips. Once you experience it, you don't forget it.

Practice Exercise: Intuition

This exercise is like a double blind medical experiment in which neither the doctor nor the patient knows whether the patient is receiving a drug or a placebo. It's adapted from Laura Day's excellent book, *Practical Intuition*. You're going to be answering a question that I've asked, which is at the bottom of page 173. Don't peek!

Take a few minutes to get comfortable and make sure that you won't be disturbed for ten or fifteen minutes. Breathe deeply and relax. Now look at the list of words below and write one sentence that uses each word. The sentences can be long or short, simple or complex, silly or logical; it doesn't matter. There aren't any right or wrong answers.

1. Stars _____

2. My childhood _____

3. My spouse (or significant other) _____

4. My career _____

5. My home _____

6. My kids _____

7. My creativity _____

8. I dream _____

9. I hope _____

10. I wish _____

11. My ideal life is _____

Read through your responses as though you've
written two or three paragraphs of prose. As you
read the question and think about your responses
to the list, does your body feel different anywhere?

Do you experience a flush of heat or maybe a chill in any part of your body? Do you feel a tightness or an ache in any part of your body?

Jot down any physical or emotional responses you're experiencing. Record anything that zips through your mind—images, thoughts, whatever.

My Responses

_____

_____

_____

_____

_____

_____

The question you answered is: How can astrology improve my life?

Children and Astrology

Robert Hand wrote what is probably the best book on kids and the stars. *Planets in Youth: Patterns in Early Development* takes the reader through every possible facet of natal astrology but applies it to children. In his introduction, he explains his concept of what children are and how he tailored his book to coincide with his perceptions.

"I prefer to assume, and my observations as a parent and teacher confirm this, that children have exactly the same needs and drives as adults, that they are neither virtuous nor bestial and that they do whatever will allow them to survive, both as biological entities and as personalities."

The ultimate test with any astrology book is to test the content with someone you know well. I read the portions of Hand's book that apply to my daughter's chart and found his observations to be quite accurate. He is never fatalistic about his interpretations and approaches his interpretations with the understanding that the natal chart is only a blueprint to be molded and sculpted through free will.

When interpreting a child's chart, it's important to follow several guidelines:

1. Put a positive spin on your interpretation. If you see something negative in the chart, express it as something to be aware of and not as something cast in stone.
2. Emphasize the element of free will.
3. Attempt to illustrate how a child's talents and abilities can be enhanced.
4. Never predict illness or death, even if the aspects seem to lean in that direction.

CHAPTER 3

Roundup

Relocating

L et's say you want to move, but aren't sure
which area of the country would suit you.
One way to gain insight into the issue is
to do a relocation chart.

A relocation chart is done by using your
date and time of birth with the longitude and
latitude for the place you might move to. If the
city isn't far from your place of birth, the differ-
ences between the two charts will be small. But
if a considerable distance is involved, the house
cusps will change, which will also alter the
placement of the planets in the houses.

The value in this is to choose a place where the planet placements emphasize your areas of interest. If you want to make more money, for instance, then you might benefit from a Jupiter place- ment in the second house. If you want to be more creative, then Jupiter in the fifth house might be better.

Transit Charts

This type of chart shows where the planets are at a particular time, day, and place. It's usually run concurrently with a natal chart and is intended to pinpoint patterns that are happening on a given day and shows how these patterns impact your natal chart.

With a transit chart, it's easy to spot broad patterns that might influence different areas of your family's life. From studying the transits to my daughter's chart, for instance, I know that when transiting Mars is crossing the cusp of her sixth or seventh house, she's more prone to colds, bronchitis, and respiratory problems in general. I know that when a Moon in Cancer transits my fourth house, I'm not in the mood to be away from home. When it's transiting my Midheaven, I usually experience conflicts between my home life and career.

The slower-moving planets exert influence for longer periods of times in transit charts. So if you're running weekly transits to your natal chart, you won't see much change in the areas they affect. But the faster-moving planets can be used for insight into daily events and situations.

Horary Astrology

This type of astrology is geared to answer specific questions. You can ask virtually anything. How's your job interview next week going to go? Where are your lost keys? How soon is your house going to sell? The first house or Ascendant represents the person asking the question and the issue you're asking about is found in the house that rules that issue. You use the ruling planet of each house and look for aspects these planets make to the Moon.

Horary astrology has hundreds of rules and I don't recommend using it until you've mastered the basics of natal astrology.

Election Charts

Are you getting married soon? Staring a business?
Planning a vacation? Then an election chart may
be just what you need to guide you about timing.

They are similar to horary charts, but with
variations on the rules. Again, I recommend
using them only after you've grasped the basics
of natal astrology.

Progressions

If you want to know the broad patterns you'll
be dealing with for the next year, then a progressed chart can shed light on the situation. A
progressed chart is an update of your natal
horoscope and the two should be read
together. There are, however, many ways to do
progressions and I recommend a thorough
grounding in the basics before you attempt it.

Medical and Mundane Astrology

These two types of astrology are very specialized. Medical astrologers should be thoroughly versed in physiology, nutrition, anatomy, and medicine in general. Unless a medical astrologer is licensed to practice medicine, however, he or she can only diagnose. This type of astrology can be valuable in uncovering hidden factors in illness.

Mundane astrology concerns world events—economy, wars, conflicts, elections, weather patterns, current events, anything that impacts a nation.

Predictive Astrology

There are a number of excellent books on the market that cover the specific types of astrology.

The classic book on transits is *Planets in Transit: Life Cycle for Living,* by Robert Hand.

Sasha Fenton's book, *Predicting the Future with Astrology,* covers transits, solar and lunar return charts, and progressed charts. Steven Forrest's *The Changing Sky* covers transits and progressions. It's a reader-friendly book and I recommend it for anyone studying predictive astrology.

Nancy Anne Hastings's book, *The Practice of Prediction,* covers transits, secondary progressions, and solar arcs. Like Forrest's book, it's user friendly.

The Only Way to . . . series by Marion D. March and Joan McEvers covers all types of predictive astrology, with ample examples so that even the beginner can grasp the concepts.

Astrology, the Famous, and the Infamous

Dante used astrology. So did Teddy Roosevelt, Mark Twain, Shakespeare, Benjamin Franklin, Sir Francis Bacon, Hitler, Ronald Reagan, J. Paul Getty, and Winston Churchill.

Hitler was such an advocate of astrology that he coerced famed astrologer Wilhelm Wulff into casting horoscopes for the Third Reich. Yet, he banned its practice in Germany, presumably so no one else would have access to the information that he did. In his book *Zodiac and the Swastika,* Wulff quoted Heinrich Himmler as saying, "We cannot permit any astrologer to follow their calling except those who are working for us."

The media launched into a feeding frenzy when it was discovered that Nancy Reagan had been consulting an astrologer to determine the timing of her husband's public moves. But as astrologer Sydney Omarr noted, "Ronald Reagan is not the first California governor or president to use astrology. The signing of the Declaration of Independence very likely was timed by astrology. Most of the signers, including Thomas Jefferson, were familiar with astrology."

Using Astrology with Other Divinatory Tools

As a divinatory tool, astrology is sometimes used in conjunction with tarot spreads—the way the tarot cards are laid out in a reading. Twelve cards are selected that represent an astrological house or area of your life.

The first card would relate to everything that concerns you personally; it would be analogous to the ascendant. The second card relates to your material resources and money. The third house relates to your siblings, friends, neighbors,  the way you communicate, and short journeys.

If the cards are laid out in two straight lines, with six in the first row and six in the second, it's easy to spot certain aspects. Oppositions, for instance, would be seen in cards one and seven, two and eight, and so on through the houses. A trine, for instance, would be cards four, eight, and twelve.

The astrological spread is excellent for a yearly reading.

Spiritual Astrology

Most astrologers acknowledge a spiritual dimension in horoscope interpretation. But authors Jan Spiller and Karen McCoy took the idea to new heights in their book *Spiritual Astrology*.

Their premise is that solar and lunar eclipses that occurred prenatally are significant to the individual. In McCoy's analysis of four thousand charts, she discovered that ". . . for the vast majority of people, the sign of their solar eclipse indicated lessons they had come to teach their fellow beings, while the sign of the lunar eclipse guided them to the lessons they needed to learn in order to continue their own soul growth."

They provide an ephemeris in their book

that lists the date of every solar and lunar eclipse since the turn of the century. You locate the eclipse that occurred immediately before your birthdate, then look in the text to determine what it means.

When I tried it, I found that the solar eclipse that occurred closest to my birthdate of June 7, 1947, was on May 20, 1947. It was in Taurus, at 28'42". The lunar eclipse closest to my birthdate occurred on June 3, 1947, in Sagittarius at 12'22". This would place the solar eclipse in my seventh house of partnerships and the lunar eclipse in my second house of material resources.

"Through you, your fellow beings can learn a proper prosperity consciousness," McCoy writes under the heading for solar eclipses in Taurus. "You are also here to teach the importance of having strong spiritual values." Since this eclipse falls in my seventh house, it suggests this will happen in my intimate partnerships.

What I find particularly interesting about this description is that I'm married to a Taurus, who is also a writer. We are each other's first editors and have collaborated on metaphysical books.

Under the description for Sagittarius in lunar eclipses, the authors write: "You have come into his life to break all prejudices and to learn to understand the common thread that runs through all forms of philosophy, religion, and spirituality." These are themes that I often explore in my fiction and the general description certainly resonates for me.

Much of the research into esoteric facets of astrology involves unconventional tools—like hypnotic regression, meditation, and intuition. These very tools often come under attack simply because they aren't the norm. As Spiller notes, "There are many nonmaterial realities that have very definite physical effects. Gravity is not visible, yet its existence is self-evident. In the same way the final 'proof' of astrology's validity is whether or not it can be of practical use in your life."

Astrology Software

If you're in the market for an astrology software program, by all means search the web before you buy. Many software companies offer free demos that you can download or view online. I found this particular feature extremely helpful when I was looking for an astrology software program. I knew what I needed, what I could afford, and found it.

Astrology software covers a vast spectrum in prices. You can pick up Xpert's astrology software program for about $10. It's very basic, with a limited atlas, and planet degrees and configurations that are sometimes inaccurate. But it's a good place to start because it's simple to use.

For years, I used an Astro program that did the job well and efficiently, but wasn't user friendly. I supplemented this with Xpert's software, which did transits quickly, but couldn't do progressions.

At the other end of the spectrum lies Solar Fire, touted by some astrologers and damned by others. It costs about $200.

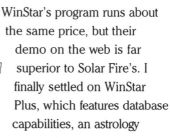

WinStar's program runs about the same price, but their demo on the web is far superior to Solar Fire's. I finally settled on WinStar Plus, which features database capabilities, an astrology tutor, and midpoint dials, and computes virtually any kind of chart you can think of.

Astrology in Cyberspace

One of the beauties of the information highway is the immediacy of information. Tomorrow's horoscope is as accessible as the planetary positions for the month or year, the meaning of obscure astrological details, or the chart of a recently deceased celebrity. Choose your search engine, type in the word you're looking for, hit the SEARCH button, and you're off.

To get to the astrology sites on the Web, you need either a URL (Uniform Resource Locator—a Web address), or a good search engine or both. DejaNews is the best of the metaphysical search engines. By plugging in a word or phrase, it takes you to where you want to go. If you use astrology as your search word, you'll find an ever-changing list of astrology sites. In 1998, this list included NewAge.com; Astrology Metalog; the Astrology Zone; AstroLife Home Page; the Internet Oracle; Vedic Astrology; Quincunx Astrology Applied; and Astrology.Net.

The oldest astrology newsgroups on the Web are at Alt.astrology, started in 1991. It offers a wealth of information in its FAQ (frequently asked questions) section. But it's inundated with ads (spam) and many of the links to other astrology sites are obsolete. It's screaming for a housecleaning.

At astrologr.com you'll find Tess Reitma's newsgroups and mailing lists information for astrology. Here, too, is a link to Metalog, which will take you to the Astrological Association of Great Britain. Metalog's Web page has a directory of astrologers that lists practitioners worldwide. At www.exotique.com/fringe/astrology.htm, you'll find an extensive list of astrology sites.